PLAYING IT SAFE

For Bee,
my personal safety hazard

WARNING

Imagine a world where you were banned from baking your granny a cake or feeding your child toast. Welcome to Britain in the 21st century, where the Jobsworth now lords it large, issuing edicts of mind-boggling stupidity that ruin the quality of people's lives all in the name of Health and Safety.

In 1998, the Lord Chancellor ended Legal Aid for personal injury claims and recommended that all future claimants seek redress through 'no win, no fee' legal firms. The floodgates opened, and now it is barely possible to watch commercial television in Britain without being asked, 'Have you had a trip or fall anywhere?'

We now live in a world where council workmen legally vandalise the graves of people's loved ones, and where Wellington boots come with a 24-page instruction manual. There is virtually no area of our lives left untouched by the Health and Safety brigade, a group that has banned even more commonplace activities than the Taliban have.

Today, the most innocuous events, from the egg-and-spoon race to a choir performance, require risk assessment. Our society is so wrapped up in 'compensation culture' that even the chairman of the Health and Safety Commission, Bill Callaghan, clearly concedes that the British way of life is being ruined by over-zealous use of Health and Safety laws, with petty bureaucrats taking all the fun out of life.

Playing it Safe lets us laugh at ourselves and at the daft predicament we have placed ourselves in. But be warned: if you read this book it will be taken as tacit agreement not to seek compensation from the author, editors, publisher or distributors in the event of a paper-cut, repetitive strain injury, or simply a rupture from laughing at the absurd state of Britain today.

Alan Pearce
www.alanpearce.com

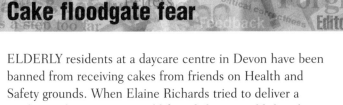

ELDERLY residents at a daycare centre in Devon have been banned from receiving cakes from friends on Health and Safety grounds. When Elaine Richards tried to deliver a Madeira cake to a 96-year-old friend she was told that the cake contained unknown ingredients that might cause illness in those who ate it. Age Concern, which runs the centre, could be sued, they added. Mrs Richards of Braunton, North Devon, a lifelong member of the Women's Institute, said: 'My cakes are perfectly healthy, baked with the finest natural ingredients. I've been making cakes for 60 years and have fed a family of four on my cooking. The worst they've had is a bit of indigestion from eating too much.' But Andrea Scott, regional director of Age Concern, said food regulation guidelines had to be followed: 'We have very many elderly and frail people that attend daycare and some are diabetic. If I let one person do this,' she said, 'it will open the floodgates.'

Daily Mail 2/6/06

Beware, falling pears!

TOWN hall chiefs have made themselves a laughing stock after cordoning off two pear trees in case their fruit falls on people. The 30 ft trees have stood in a city park for 50 years without any problems. But now a team of council workmen has put up security tape and a plastic barrier to stop anyone going near them. And signs have been screwed to each tree saying: 'Warning, pears falling!' Officials acted after receiving a complaint that the trees are a health hazard. They fear the council could be sued if anyone is injured by a pear in Cripplegate Park, St John's, Worcester. The trees produce large black pears, which are the symbol of Worcestershire. But local people say they bear fruit every year and no one has ever been hurt. Barry Cox, 40, said: 'This is a crazy waste of time and money. It seems people aren't credited with common sense any more. Next thing they will be issuing people with hard hats before they enter the park.'

The Sun 4/10/06

Sitting instructions

GREATER Manchester Fire Service has drawn up a four-page safety manual to instruct crews on how to sit in a reclining chair. Firemen hoping for a rest between call-outs are banned from using the £400 device until they have been trained to do so. The first task will be to take out their 'personal-issue head protector' and place it on the back of the chair. Then, and only then, can they begin their descent, a process that must end with them sitting 'fully back'. Those who get this far can 'get ready to recline'. The manual advises: 'To release the mechanism (i.e. to start reclining), simply lift the lever under the right-hand arm of the chair (when seated). This moves the chair into its semi-reclined position (i.e. feet up, head up).' Crews are warned that only 'trained personnel' can carry out 'lubrication of mechanisms', and that sleeping bags must not be used. They are also given advice on how to deal with spillages: 'tissue should firstly be placed on the stain to absorb excess liquid', and warned that horseplay involving recliners is deemed a disciplinary offence. The fire service has spent £130 000 on its new Calcot recliners, which will be used as beds during night shifts. A fire service spokesman said: 'Training will be given for Health and Safety reasons. There are moving parts.'

Daily Telegraph 28/1/06

Eating out

TRADITIONAL cheese and onion sandwiches, known locally in the Black Country as cobs, have been taken off a pub menu after 80 years of healthy eating. The Clingfilm-wrapped cobs were banned from sale when inspectors raised concerns that they were not refrigerated. The move ended years of tradition at the old-fashioned Beacon Hotel. Stunned by the decision, drinkers gathered 90 names on a protest petition in just four days. Landlord John Hughes said: 'We've got these English pubs and there's nothing like them anywhere in the world. Tourists come and are amazed by the original features, and the cheese and onion cobs are a little part of that heritage. We keep the pub like a museum, and I feel we could have got away without a fridge.'

Wolverhampton Express and Star 15/2/07

Bags of no fun

WHEN children tumble over in the sack race, they tend to suffer nothing worse than wounded pride. But after seven years without mishap, the event has been banned from a community's annual festival because of fears that there could be legal action if anyone is injured. Organisers claim the compensation culture has led to soaring insurance premiums, which have put the activity off limits. Despite the event attracting more than 2000 young contestants each year, they say they have no alternative but to cancel it.

The insurance bill for the fun day has risen from £400 to £600 in a year, and would double if traditional events such as the sack race, three-legged dash and egg-and-spoon race were still included.

This is London 7/2/07

Nurse in danger ride

A district nurse has been banned from cycling on her patient rounds because bosses think it is too dangerous. Kathy Archer did up to 15 miles a day, which saved her employers £1000 a year in petrol and kept her fit. But Bournemouth Primary Care Trust said the traditional transport left her at risk of attack from drug users because she carries syringes and needles. They also said she could spread infection between homes as she carries all her equipment with her. But a Royal College of Nursing adviser called the decision 'nonsense.' Kathy said: 'The patients thought it was great. They were a bit surprised, but very supportive. You can take nearly everything patients need.'

Nursing Standard Magazine 9/05

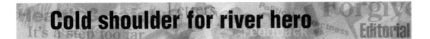
Cold shoulder for river hero

A man who has saved more than 1500 people from drowning has been told that police can no longer work with him because he is in breach of Health and Safety regulations.

George Parsonage, 61, has plied the River Clyde in Glasgow for nearly 50 years. He even received a special lifetime achievement award from Princess Alexandra. But the future of his rescue missions has been thrown into doubt by a decision by Strathclyde Police to cease all contact with him. The force said that it had taken its decision for Health and Safety reasons, after learning that Mr Parsonage's assistant had left. However, Mr Parsonage insisted that he would still rescue people from the water, but questioned the 'practicalities' of Strathclyde Police's decision. 'The police won't call me. But, if a member of the public calls and there's someone out in the river, I'll be out there. If I see someone, I'll go.'

The Times 6/5/05

Toddler's hoodie ban

A grandmother has branded as 'pathetic and laughable' a shop's policy on hoodies after her two-year-old grandson was asked to remove his hood. Brenda Cowper, 54, told how her husband took the youngster to his corner shop on a cold and windy night. 'No sooner had they got inside than the shop-keeper asked my husband to remove the little boy's hood. 'My husband said, "He's only two-and-a-half. I don't think he's going to rob you".' In November, a middle-aged nurse was refused her morning paper at the same shop for wearing a hooded lambswool cardigan. Mrs Cowper added: 'I can understand their point because there are a lot of kids that cause trouble down there, but when it's a two-year-old it's a bit pathetic and I think most people would just think it's laughable really.' Staff at the Monkton Road Stores said no one was available to comment.

York Evening Press 22/1/07

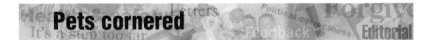

Noisy neighbours

RUGBY Council has ordered a man to move a tiny windchime from his back garden following an investigation that cost more than £1000. David Bavington was stunned to receive an official letter claiming that the 1-inch diameter chime was a 'statutory nuisance' following a complaint. And he was warned he had to take it down – or be served with a noise abatement order and face legal action. Ironically Mr Bavington, 57, and his wife Sheila bought the chime to create a feeling of calm while they were sitting in the garden of their £300 000 detached home in Ryton-on-Dunsmore, Warwickshire, with noisy airliners flying overhead on final approach to Coventry airport just over a mile away. Instead, it has landed them in a two-month legal row with officials at Rugby.

Retired sales executive Mr Bavington said: 'You can't even hear the chime if you go inside the house. But the council said there had been a complaint from someone who was annoyed by the tinkling. I told them it was ridiculous. Sending around officers to listen to a tiny windchime is a complete waste of taxpayers' money.'

Evening Standard 6/1/07

Pets cornered

MORE and more primary schools are being forced to give up school pets to avoid breaching the Department for Education's guidelines on Health and Safety. Rules say pupils must cover cuts before handling animals, wash their hands afterwards, and not put into their mouths pens, fingers or crayons that might have come into contact with the pets or their cages. But teachers say that these rules are impossible to uphold in a class of 30 children.

Daily Mirror 28/2/05

Clean Marines

HEALTH and Safety inspectors are turning their attention to the training of Britain's armed services and suggest that chlorine should be used to ensure that the water in an assault course tunnel used by Marines is nice and clean. They also recommended that handrails should be provided to stop the trainees slipping on the muddy training slopes.

Harrow Times 13/2/04

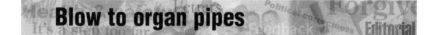

Blow to organ pipes

THE organs at Salisbury Cathedral, St Paul's in London and Birmingham Town Hall may be silenced under an EU directive aimed at limiting the amount of lead in electrical items. The regulations permit electrical equipment to have a maximum of 0.1 per cent of their weight as lead. Organ pipes have a lead content of 50 per cent or more. The directive, which seeks to minimise the amount of 'hazardous waste' that finds its way into landfill after electrical products are scrapped, would also bring to an end the 1000-year-old craft of organ building. In Britain there are about 70 companies employing about 800 people, and all their jobs are at risk. Lead is used in organ pipes because of its malleability and the distinctive sound it produces. Organists are baffled that they have been caught up in EU red tape because when organs are rebuilt the lead is not thrown away: it is re-used in new or different pipes. Katherine Venning, President of the Institute of British Organ Building, said: 'There is a very black cloud on the horizon. Pipe makers live to a ripe old age, with no known damage to their health. Pipe organs last indefinitely, and present no threat to the environment.'

The Times 18/3/06

Residents cross

RESIDENTS of an Angus village say they have been cut off from vital services by Network Rail, all in the name of safety. The level crossing near their homes at East Haven, near Carnoustie, has been padlocked. The closure is part of a new policy to prevent public access to what the company classes as private level crossings. And despite assurances from Network Rail, residents fear that they could be left high and dry if they need an ambulance. Fifty people live in the 20

houses between the railway and the sea at East Haven. They
get to their homes by car under a low bridge, but until now
larger delivery vans and vehicles such as ambulances have
used the level crossing.

BBC News 21/8/03

Moving the goal posts

WHAT'S white, wide and waist-high, but still potentially
invisible? The answer, according to a county council, is a set
of goalposts used by children playing football. They ordered
their removal from the small field where they were standing –
in case walkers fell over them. Astonished local people were
told that ramblers using a public footpath across the field might
have their heads bent over a map and not see the obstacle.
Then, of course, there was the danger to people out at night.
But the decision by Cheshire County Council has been
branded an own goal by families whose children use the field
in Alderley Edge. Philip Reid, a father of three, said: 'Councils
are constantly bleating about the obesity problem our children
are facing and then they go and mess about with facilities
aimed at combating it.' The fate of the goalposts was sealed
after an inspection by county council officials. They ordered
Macclesfield Borough Council, which owns the field, to move
them. One consolation for local people is that Macclesfield
Council is planning to improve the play area and will be
consulting them before deciding what to put there. In the
meantime, walkers can stride fearlessly across the site – so
long as they can see their way past the basketball net, swings,
slide and seesaw that are still there.

Daily Mail 23/2/07

Revolver peril

STAFF at the BBC in Birmingham have been sent a memo
advising them on how to get through a revolving door. An email
sent to 800 staff – complete with matchstick man diagrams
for ease of understanding – comes after one worker trapped
her foot in the new doors at the BBC's Birmingham studios,
cracking a toenail. 'Follow these simple steps each time you
use the doors,' says the memo entitled Revolving Security
Door User Instructions. 'To enter the secure space move
directly into the revolving door compartment. The door will
start automatically. One person per compartment. Keep
hands, feet and bags away from the edges of the door.' A BBC
spokesman said: 'We are keeping in line with the Health and
Safety at Work Act.' Employees at BBC Radio Sheffield had
previously been instructed on how to get through the peril-laden
task of boiling a kettle.

BBC insider 2/07

Fear of floating

FOAM floats have been banned from swimming pools
because of fears that children and adults could accidentally
be whacked by them. Council bosses introduced the rule
after complaints that people had been struck by the swimming
aids. But the move was branded 'mad' by parents and
swimmers using the pools in Dudley, Halesowen and
Stourbridge in the West Midlands. Mum Jill Andrews, of
Brierley Hill, was told that her son Reece, eight, could not
use his float. She said: 'I couldn't believe it. How am I
meant to teach my son to swim?' Dudley Council

spokesman Jan Jennings said: 'This decision was made for Health and Safety reasons after complaints.'

The Sun 14/6/06

Seesaw no more

AFTER almost 40 years the folk of picturesque Cotswold village Bledington were told their seesaw would have to be pulled up. It was, claimed a Playing Fields Association official, a danger under EU directive EN1176-1;1998 Playground Equipment For Outside Use. The fact that no-one had ever been hurt playing on it did not matter a jot. And the madness didn't end there. The swings also had to be moved because there was the potential risk that they could damage a child's eyes because they faced the sun.

Daily Mirror 28/2/05

Public protection basket case

FOR the last seven years Ian Collins has adorned the front of the Ring of Bells pub with a stunning display of hanging baskets and window boxes. The greenfingered publican has won numerous prizes, including Prettiest Village Pub on four occasions, and his efforts have attracted visitors from around the world. But now the 47-year-old has been forced to cancel his pub's prize-winning flower display following a visit from the local council.

Health and Safety officials claimed the hanging and wall-mounted baskets and pots were dangerous, as some of the petunias and begonias spilled onto the pavement and walkers would have had to step into the road to avoid them. The officials also claimed Mr Collins's baskets were hanging below the 8.2 ft minimum height laid down by Health and Safety regulations and people could bang their heads on them. Disappointed Mr Collins, who has run the pub in the Somerset village of Norton Fitzwarren for 12 years, claimed it was a case of 'nanny state' meddling: 'I have done this for seven years and I have never heard any complaints – in fact, it has been just the opposite.' But the county council defended its decision. Spokesman Jan Hookings said: 'The safety of the public has to be our first priority.'

Daily Mail 11/7/05

Toddle charge

THIRTY children under three years of age in Poole, Dorset, managed to raise £142 for charity by staging a 'toddlethon' through the park. They were then charged £36 by the council for checking whether the event needed policing.

Derbygripe.co.uk 2/07

Trafalgar Squares

PLASTIC signs have been put up in Trafalgar Square's fountains, banning visitors from paddling in the water. The signs, branded 'tacky' by critics, have appeared 160 years after the first fountains were built on the site. The ban spells the end for an age-old tradition of cooling down in the square's waters on a hot summer's day – often after a few drinks. Some of Britain's finest hours, including VE Day and football and rugby World Cup victories, have also been celebrated there. The signs – four in each of the two fountains – state: 'Not safe for public use' and come complete with 'No Entry' symbols.

The move is thought to have been largely prompted by fears that the Greater London Authority could be sued by revellers who injure themselves slipping over in the water.

This is London 2/6/05

Police nab conker haul

THE long arm of the law has come down on a group of conker-collecting children.

When Kiya Jayne and three friends set out to collect conkers they found themselves ordered to stop by police, who confiscated the haul and handed them official 'Stop and search' forms. They had collected nearly a whole carrier bag of shiny red conkers from the tree in Littlehampton, West Sussex, when a woman police officer arrived and swiftly brought the fun to an end. The boys' mums were stunned when their children appeared bearing four slips of paper, explaining that they had been stopped and searched. Mother-of-two Diana Jayne, 41, said she could not believe what had happened to her son. 'It was absolutely ridiculous. He's only seven and I encourage him to go blackberry picking and conker picking. I used to collect conkers when I was little.' A spokesman for Sussex Police said they had responded to calls from members of the public. 'Officers were assigned to deal with the safety issue of the children playing in the road,' he said. A bag of about 100 conkers was confiscated.

Daily Mail 3/10/06

Wees ruin race

AN international cycling race has been cancelled because of fears of competitors urinating on the Hampshire roadside. The annual Havant Grand Prix was called off after a 'stalemate' was reached between police and organisers over plans for the 113-mile race. The conduct of cyclists and the safety of road users last year led police to ban the 2006 race. The event had been running for 16 years and attracted cyclists from across the globe as well as British Olympians. Inspector Howard Marrs said: 'It is unacceptable to have masses of cyclists at the side of the road urinating, and the organisers would have to address this before the race could have gone ahead.' He said the race would be stopped on safety grounds following the conduct of the riders.

BBC News 9/8/06

Paedo camera concern

PARENTS have been banned from filming and taking photographs of a school Nativity play – because of fears that paedophiles could get hold of the images. St James RC Primary in Hattersley, Tameside, is thought to be the first school in Greater Manchester to introduce such a ban. Only members of staff at the school will be allowed to take photographs, which will be made available to parents. Head teacher Barbara Robinson declined to comment in detail, but said she was following guidelines set down by the Catholic Diocese of Shrewsbury, which governs the school.

Manchester Evening News 18/12/03

Cancer banner banned

A cancer awareness banner was removed by a council because of fears that it might damage a lamp post. Macmillan Cancer Relief said: 'We were told it was a very ornate and important post.' The council in Bury St Edmunds, Suffolk, once banned hanging baskets.

The People 12/2/06

Don't do the conger

A madcap contest in which men slap each other with a dead eel has been banned on health and taste grounds after just one complaint. Conger Cuddling is a kind of human skittles which has raised thousands for the Royal National Lifeboat

Institution. Rival teams knock each other off small boxes by battering them with a 5 ft conger swinging from a rope. But locals are furious after RNLI chiefs had to axe this year's event over the single protest. The killjoy protestor claimed it was disrespectful to dead animals. Richard Fox, 67, who invented the sport 32 years ago, fumed: 'It's the most ludicrous thing I've ever heard. How can you be disrespecting an animal's rights when it is dead?'

The Sun 29/7/06

Mince pie madness

ORGANISERS of a village Christmas party have been told they must carry out a risk assessment of their mince pies – or their festivities will be cancelled. Council bosses say posters will have to be displayed at the party in Embsay, in the Yorkshire Dales, warning villagers that the pies contain nuts and suet pastry. The cocoa content and temperature of the hot chocolate must also be checked. Resident Steve Dobson said the rules had made the small party as difficult to arrange as the Great Yorkshire Show. Mr Dobson said he learned of the regulations after writing to Craven District Council to ask if he could use a car park outside Embsay village hall to hold the free party for the community. 'It is bureaucracy gone mad,' Mr Dobson said. 'The council gave me a huge list of things we had to do. I wrote back, a little bit tongue in cheek, asking if I really had to risk assess free mince pies and a brass band, and they said 'yes'. Everything we do, from putting tinsel up to providing refreshments, has to be assessed. We have to consider the dangers involved, that someone might choke on their mince pie, or have a nut allergy. I also understand that Santa may need a Criminal Records Bureau check.'

BBC News 4/12/06

Getting the wind down

BRITAIN'S biggest offshore windfarm has been shut down because it was too windy. Prime Minister Tony Blair heralded the opening of the 30-turbine North Hoyle windfarm, off the coast of Rhyl, as the 'foundation' of the country's move towards renewable energy. But the operators of North Hoyle, National Wind Power, admitted they had to turn off the turbines to protect them from 70 mph winds. Anti-windfarm campaigners described the move as absurd, saying surely the turbines should operate more effectively the windier the weather. National Wind Power's development manager for Wales, Mark Legerton, said: 'There are a few days of the year in which the turbines don't operate to protect them from heavy loading, which they would otherwise receive in the high winds.

Derbygripe.co.uk 2/07

Bacon buttie cancer worry

BARMY health experts are warning that eating bacon can give you cancer. A bladder tumour link was found in people tucking into the treat five times a week. The Sun's own GP, Dr Carol Cooper, played down the scare: 'If you look at anything closely enough, eating tons of it would be bad for your health. Lots of people will read this and think they must not go near bacon, which would be wrong.' The daft bacon warning follows a series of killjoy food scares. The bacon research followed the diets of 135 000 adults and found a 59 per cent increased risk of bladder cancer in those who ate excessive amounts of bacon.

The Sun 29/11/0

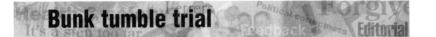

Home smoke ban

CRAZY council bosses want staff to report people who smoke in their own homes and refuse to stub out their cigarettes. The barmy idea, dreamed up by Health and Safety chiefs, is revealed in a Birmingham City Council memo leaked to the Sunday Mercury.

It says that staff, such as social workers and home helps, could be at risk from passive smoking during house visits. The memo orders employees to tell tenants, including pensioners or housebound residents, to put out their ciggies – or face being reported.

The memo at the centre of the controversy was circulated by Viv Strong, the council's Directorate Safety Officer, and is titled Corporate Policy on Smoking. It reads: 'Where the service user refuses to cooperate, the employee should report this incident immediately to their manager. Upon receipt of such information managers should review the risk assessment.' But one council insider said: 'This is about as daft as you can get. If some official walked into Dot Cotton's home in EastEnders and told her to stub out her fag, it would be dismissed by viewers as too far-fetched.'

Sunday Mercury 10/10/04

Bunk tumble trial

A prisoner is suing jail bosses for negligence – after he fell off the top bunk in his cell. Gerry Cooper cut his head after rolling out of bed while asleep at Bullingdon Prison, near

Bicester, Oxfordshire. He claims that cons' beds breach Health and Safety regulations. In a letter to a prisoners' magazine, Cooper says bunk beds are 'an accident waiting to happen'. He says his governor told him inmates who felt unsafe in top bunks need not sleep in one. The Prison Service denied that was a policy.

The People 3/9/06

Home-coming hazard

KILLJOY council bosses are under fire for wrecking a war hero's homecoming. Wounded Para Ricky Trueman, 20, arrived back from Iraq on crutches to find his family home festooned with yellow ribbons, balloons and banners. The bunting stretched 50 yards either side of his parents' bungalow and was draped high across the road. Ricky almost burst into tears when he saw it. But highway chiefs in Doncaster, South Yorks, were less impressed. A Jobsworth official turned up at the street three days later and ordered the bunting to be taken down because it was a 'safety hazard'. Disgusted mum Michelle, 42, said: 'How can anyone be so insensitive after all Ricky has been through? The bunting stretched across the road but was so high even the dustbin lorry could pass underneath.' She added: 'Ricky fought for Queen and country and came home injured – he deserves better than this.' Ricky suffered shrapnel wounds in a landmine blast while serving as a private with 3 Para near Basra. He said: 'After what I've been through it leaves a bad taste. All people wanted to do was welcome me home, but all the council can think about are their rules and regulations.'

The Sun 13/5/03

Lunch time no booze

ANGRY town hall staff claim they have been stopped from
supping a lunchtime pint. Unison says the ban on work-hours'
drinking in Hackney, London, is 'draconian' and affects all
3700 staff. But the council said it only applied where safety
was an issue.

The People 2/4/06

Chop for city trees

A London council has caused a furore after threatening to cut
down one in five of its trees on grounds of cost and safety.
Ealing Council says the 4500 lime trees are too expensive to
maintain and are the cause of large insurance payouts because
of the 'compensation culture'. But this has provoked fury from
residents and environmentalists, who fear the borough's repu-
tation as the 'queen of the suburbs' will be destroyed. Council

leader John Cudmore claims the trees are a problem because of their 'vigorous' growth and attraction to insects, whose droppings made pavements slippery. He said the limes looked like 'cabbages on sticks' because they have to be severely pruned back every three years. He said the council received 'many, many complaints from residents' and said a radical solution was needed.

This is London 20/2/07

Pricks out

COUNCILLOR Dick Barker, from Belton, Norfolk, is calling for his village's rose bushes to be dug up in case they harm children.

Derbygripe.co.uk 2/07

No outings for schools

TEACHERS' union NASUWT sparked fury when it called for a ban on school trips.

General Secretary Chris Keates said his members should abandon outings because society was becoming 'increasingly litigious'. So great are the concerns that staff at Airyhall Primary in Aberdeen cancelled a residential break to Perthshire to mark pupils' final year. The treat, which had become a school tradition, included physical activities such as mountain biking, kayaking and orienteering at the Dalguise Centre near Dunkeld. And in Derby education chiefs advised schools not to take children to sunny places in case they get skin cancer.

Daily Mirror 28/2/05

High stakes

TRAPEZE artists have been told to start wearing hard hats to comply with new EU safety rules. Jugglers, tightrope walkers and other acrobats have also been instructed to don safety headgear because of European regulations covering workers employed at heights greater than the average stepladder.

Daily Telegraph 23/7/06

Don't rub the scouts

SCOUT leaders have been condemned after it was revealed they had banned helpers from putting suncream on youngsters – unless they are already suffering from sunburn. The Scout Association issued the diktat in the hope of preventing allegations of child abuse.

But it explained that the ban did not apply if Cubs and Scouts were already burned – because they are considered to be patients in need of first aid. The policy was slammed by parents and campaigners. Father-of-three Richard Stevenson said: 'I asked what sort of activities they would be getting up to. When I heard it was abseiling and shooting I thought, this is great – just the sort of thing that the safety culture normally precludes.' A spokesman for the Scout Association confirmed that leaders could not apply suncream to children: 'If a child is responsible enough to go away on their own to a camp, then they are responsible enough to apply suncream. We have strict child protection policies to make sure no adult is putting themselves or any young person at risk.'

Daily Mail 5/8/06

23

Village pond hazard

VILLAGERS have hit out at 'ridiculous' plans to fence off their pond so that no one falls in. Health and Safety experts said the 'water hazard' in exclusive West Itchenor, near Chichester, should have fencing around one side and a sign warning of the dangers of deep water. The pond is a home for ducks, carp and a water vole. It has a bench along one side and is popular with families who visit to feed the ducks. The bombshell was dropped on residents in a parish newsletter which declared: 'As a parish council we are obliged to undertake risk assessments in the village and have been doing so for the past 20 months.' Council chairperson Louise Goldsmith said the local authority had an obligation under the Occupiers' Liability Act. 'We realised we were not covered by insurance on the pond. We as a council own 50 per cent of it and lease the other 50 per cent. We were advised by our insurers that we should have a risk assessment. We have had to do this. We have not made this up.' But village resident James Wilkinson said: 'It does all seem a bit ridiculous. As far as I know the pond has a good accident record in that nobody has been hurt there. It is more of a muddy puddle than a big open pond.'

Brighton Argus 28/11/06

Prescott turns down the heat

THE Deputy Prime Minister's nanny state will plumb new depths by controlling the heat of water in our tubs. Mr Prescott has ordered that special taps which limit the temperature be fitted in all homes built from next year. He says the law is 'essential' to stop the rising tide of scalding accidents, insisting the new home safety regulations will protect the young, elderly and infirm who fall into piping-hot baths. But the special valves would also stop people topping up with hot water when enjoying a long soak. And residents would be forced to pay for annual inspections to make sure they are working properly.

Aides confirmed regulations could be extended to force owners of existing homes to fit the mixer devices. Furious plumbers and the Tories urged Mr Prescott to wash the 'crazy' plan down the plughole. Richard Nissen, a London plumber, said: 'This is legislation gone mad. It is going to mean a lot of angry customers because of the cost of installing these valves and carrying out the mandatory annual inspections. You won't be able to warm up your bath with extra water as the temperature will be regulated by the valve. It's ludicrous.'

The Sun 16/5/05

Caution over Custard

CUSTARD the cat has been banned from a council building – because bosses say he is a Health and Safety risk. Stuart Dawson, manager at the housing benefit office in Dorchester, Dorset, says some staff are allergic to cats and others might trip over Custard.

But one worker said: 'It's a barmy decision. He brought karma here.'

The People 31/12/06

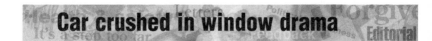

Gormless art ban

ART lovers reacted with dismay and fury to a decision to remove Antony Gormley's celebrated installation, Another Place, from a Merseyside beach on the grounds that it was a Health and Safety risk. Planners at Sefton Council demanded the installation's removal. Sailors might founder if they struck one of the so-called 'tin men', they said, while children, trying to swim out to the most far-flung statues, were in danger of being cut off by incoming tides. Supporters of Another Place acknowledge that the installation, which has attracted 600 000 visitors since it was secured to the sea bed in July 2005, was always intended to be a temporary piece of art. Laurie Peake, the project's manager, said: 'We were dumbstruck. The coastguard and the RNLI said they had no objections.' But Conservative councillor Debi Jones said: 'In today's litigious world I find it strange no one looked into the Health and Safety aspect. I asked the committee if they would have a clear conscience in court if a lawsuit were taken up.'

Daily Telegraph 21/10/06

Car crushed in window drama

ROGER Bugg had his motorcar towed away and crushed because he had left the windows open half an inch. The £500 Escort was destroyed by cops after a traffic warden reported it as a fire hazard. The warden said kids could have dropped a match through the windows, threatening an electricity substation. Mr Bugg said: 'If a car is dumped by all means crush it, but mine was taxed and legally parked.'

Derbygripe.co.uk 2/07

Legion in stab fear

POPPY pins are being ditched by Royal British Legion branches amid fears wearers will sue if they are injured by them. Chiefs are blaming Britain's growing compensation greed for the crazy situation leading up to Remembrance Day. Peter Westwell, secretary of the Legion's Shropshire branch, said: 'It's claims culture gone mad.' Around Britain, sellers have been ordered not to pin poppies on children, and anxious branches are extending the ban to adults. Most are now supplying stickers, plastic clasps or poppies with stems for button holes. Fund-raiser Malcolm Gainard of the Keynsham branch in Somerset said: 'People can easily stab themselves with a pin and there is the worry of litigation.'

The Sun 3/11/03

Pub lunch panned

A woman in a wheelchair has been refused entry to a Devon pub's beer garden because she is 'a fire risk.' Disabled Annette Boucher, 51, of Crediton wanted to have lunch in the garden behind the town's General Sir Redvers Buller pub with her student-nurse daughter Charlotte and friend. But after the two women had pushed the multiple sclerosis sufferer along a rough and overgrown path leading to the garden, they were told that they could not go in. Staff insisted that Mrs Boucher would be a fire risk because she would block the path in the event of an emergency. Pub chain J D Wetherspoon, which owns the pub, has since apologised and has offered mum and daughter a free meal, which they have accepted. But it is still refusing to allow Mrs Boucher into the garden.

Mult-sclerosis.org 6/8/03

Army pipers plugged

SOLDIERS learning to play the bagpipes have been told to limit their practice sessions to only 24 minutes a day, or 15 minutes when indoors. Pipers will also have to wear ear plugs under the new guidelines brought in by Health and Safety officials. The advice, aimed at preventing soldiers from suffering hearing problems, was issued after a study by the Army Medical Directorate environmental health team. Tests showed that outdoors the sound of bagpipes could reach 111 decibels, slightly louder than a pneumatic drill. Indoors, the instrument could reach 116 decibels, or as loud as a chainsaw. Bagpipes have played a crucial role in Scottish regiments, which have traditionally been led into battle by kilted pipers. Davy Garrett, who played the pipes in the Army for 12 years and now runs a piping school, said: 'This is just another example of the nanny state and one that I am very concerned could ruin the future of piping in Scotland.' Bill Lark, 85, a Black Watch piper who led his comrades into action against the Japanese in 1944, said the rules were 'ridiculous'. He said: 'The pipes should be played loudly. That's how they inspire soldiers and scare the enemy.' A spokesman for the Army in Scotland said the rules were a 'prudent precaution'.

Daily Telegraph 25/7/06

A youngster has been banned from taking sunscreen to school to protect herself in scorching weather. The decision – condemned by cancer campaigners – has even been backed by Manchester Town Hall bosses. The row flared after ten-year-old Georgia Holt was told she could not apply suncream as temperatures topped 26C at Seymour Road Primary School, in Clayton. She was told Health and Safety guidelines issued by Manchester City Council warned the creams could pose a risk to other pupils if they had allergies. Georgia's mum, Wendy, of Stokes Street, Clayton, said she was furious about the ban. 'I'm really annoyed about this,' she said. 'It was absolutely scorching and Georgia got all worked up about it and seemed quite upset.' But a Manchester City Council spokesman said: 'We believe the school acted responsibly and in accordance with the Health and Safety guidelines. We advise that children do not bring sunscreen into school or share it with other children, as some children can suffer allergic reactions to it.'

Manchester Evening News 18/7/03

Meatball in choke terror

A primary school in Stow-on-the-Wold has taken meatballs off its lunch menu in case pupils choke on them. Rebecca Scutt, the head teacher, told parents: 'It is better to be safe than sorry and we have asked for meatballs to be removed.'

Derbygripe.co.uk 2/07

NORWICH City Council is threatening to fell seven horse chestnut trees because of the risk posed by their conkers. Apparently they are a danger to pedestrians, who could slip on the mulch they leave behind. The golf-ball-sized chestnuts could also come crashing down onto passing cars, while sticks thrown by children to dislodge them could cause serious head injuries, the Council has warned. There are also fears that children gathering conkers are at risk from vehicles. Council spokeswoman Rachel Bobbitt said: 'In preparation for the removal, in recent years Norwich City Council has been planting replacement lime trees alongside, so semi-mature trees will still be on Bluebell Road when the horse chestnuts are removed,' she said. Fortunately, not all the councillors agree. Liberal Democrat Jane Roozer said: 'Everyone has gone through a period of collecting conkers and I find it quite unbelievable that we are thinking of chopping down very healthy, beautiful trees. It's just ludicrous beyond belief. At the end of the day, children will get up to mischief and we can't go cutting down all our conker trees because of the potential for accidents.'

iGreens.org.uk 14/6/01

Off your bike

THE father of a child at a Devon school is fuming at the school's refusal to allow bicycles on the premises. The move follows a new government initiative to get more children walking, cycling, and taking the bus to school in an attempt to cut congestion. But Ivybridge Community College has told pupils that bikes are banned. Paul Whiteley, of Bittaford in Devon, wants his 12-year-old son to cycle to school. He said: 'The school has told me there are issues of safety and access, but I thought education was about learning to solve problems and I don't think this school is doing enough to solve these problems. The school clearly has the health and safety of the children at heart, but I would say life is a balance of risks.' A spokesman for Devon County Council said the school was concerned that pupils on bikes would be at risk from school buses and other traffic on the narrow road leading to the school.

BBC News 19/9/03

Reprieve in swing loophole

THE children's swings in Great Somerford, removed last December over safety concerns, could be granted a reprieve because of a legal loophole. Only the swings' frame remains on the Watkins Lane play area after a report said that the chains were too long and there was a possibility that a child would swing off. Residents were up in arms when the popular children's attraction was removed. The swings have an impeccable safety record: there has not been a reported injury since they were installed in 1977. The Royal Society for the Prevention of Accidents has contacted the parish council and said that there was a possibility the village equipment could get a reprieve. Parish Clerk Mark Edwards said: 'The Society contacted us and said that their interpretation of the laws could be different and said that they would do their own inspection. I will be very interested to see what they come back with; I hope it will mean that we will be able to get the swings back.'

Swindon Advertiser 23/1/03

Sponge cake in health scare

ALL little Emma Matthews wanted to do was celebrate her sixth birthday at school with a nice chocolate sponge. But before she could divide up the tasty treat among her hungry classmates, teachers stepped in and declared the tempting confection a health risk.

Emma's parents had bought the cake in a local shop and then went to some trouble to decorate it with extra icing and chocolate buttons for the pupils at St Bride's Primary School in Bothwell, Lanarkshire. However, teachers told the astonished youngster that because the original packaging had been opened it breached Health and Safety rules and they couldn't let anyone else eat it. A note Emma brought home from school said: 'I am sorry to inform you that we are unable to use Emma's birthday cake due to the fact that it was not sealed in the box.' Emma's mother, Lorraine Matthews, 36, said she was flabbergasted by the school's actions. 'Emma came out of school carrying the cake and she was really upset,' said mother-of-two Mrs Matthews, adding: 'How could it have been safe for Emma to eat but not any of the other kids? The school never have a problem with parents preparing cakes when we are asked to make them for bring and buy sales and things like that, so why now?'

Daily Mail 18/10/06

Crackdown on kites

THE flying of stunt kites has been banned at Blackpool after a woman walking her dog became entangled in a string and was dragged to the ground. Fylde Borough Council has imposed the ban on its shoreline and open spaces, but the move has angered kite enthusiasts, who were developing the windy beaches around Blackpool as a centre for power kiting and kite surfing. The council said that people would still be allowed to fly traditional single-string kites. Phil Rawcliffe, of the British Kite Surfing Association, says enthusiasts have complied with stringent safety measures, but the council has pressed ahead with its ban without consultation. 'There is uproar about it. Since we set up a club at Blackpool we have had risk assessments and paid insurance. We have done everything by the book. Lots of cafés and bed-and-breakfast hotels are going to suffer. One man from the Midlands has cancelled a trip up with his family of four. That sort of money is going to be lost to the economy for as long as this ban is in place.'

The Times 21/4/06

Cold charity

PUPILS at a North Wales high school have been banned from wearing charity wristbands over fears for their safety. Teachers and governors at Denbigh High School said the colourful bands, which promote issues including anti-bullying, were a hazard in the classroom. The awareness bracelets have been made popular by celebrities, including footballer David Beckham. However, Denbigh High School said they contravene their rules on uniform. Head teacher Alison Duncan said the bands broke the school's policy to restrict the wearing of jewellery and also its Health and Safety rules. Clwyd Parry, chair of governors, said: 'They are very strong and very tough and could cause a hazard during PE, outside activities, arts and crafts and engineering.'

BBC News 4/3/05

No dirty visits

HOSPITAL chiefs have been branded barmy after banning
flowers and child visitors – to help them fight the MRSA
superbug. The measures were introduced after outbreaks at St
Richards in Chichester, Sussex, increased from 22 to 25 last
year. A spokeswoman said restricting visitors would help
reduce infections and no kids could call unless it was to see a
close relative. She said: 'It's about clear access to patients'
tables and being able to wipe them down.' But Jim Morrison,
whose mum is being treated for a broken foot, said: 'It's health
and safety gone mad.'

The People 22/1/06

Balloon stunt banned

THE BBC has played down reports that a promotional stunt
featuring Belfast DJ Colin Murray is too dangerous. The video, to
plug Murray's new evening show on Radio One, showed the
presenter being released skywards attached to around 500 helium
balloons. But, according to reports, the BBC decided not to show
the video in the aftermath of Top Gear presenter Richard
Hammond's 300 mph crash in a jet-powered car.

Belfast Telegraph 6/12/06

Safety slabs

HUNDREDS of gravestones have been pushed over by council
workers at cemeteries across Edinburgh as part of a city-wide

safety probe. At least 120 000 headstones and other structures within the city's 32 cemeteries are being checked as part of the safety drive. But the move has been branded 'over the top' by critics who claim there is no need for the drastic action. Under the move, any headstone deemed to be a danger will be removed and reset. If no members of family can be found to pay for reinstatement, then headstones will be left lying flat on top of the grave. But the work, which involves workmen simply leaning on the stones until they fall, has upset many visitors to Edinburgh's cemeteries. A 46-year-old local resident, who wishes to remain anonymous, said: 'I couldn't believe it when I saw two council workers leaning and pushing at the stones. When I approached the men to ask what they were doing they told me it was on grounds of safety after a little boy was killed by a gravestone in Harrogate.'

Edinburgh Evening News 24/1/03

Drinks police go soft

A school has sparked a row with parents by banning pupils from bringing in soft drinks. Governors at the south London primary school introduced the ban – which covers everything from fruit juice to fizzy drinks – because they fear high levels of sugar in some drinks could harm children's health. But some parents say it leaves their children with only one drink – water – which many do not like, and in hot weather pupils have been returning home tired, listless and dehydrated. More than 100 parents at the 390-pupil De Lucy primary school in Abbey Wood have signed a petition demanding the policy – believed to be the first of its kind in London – be reversed.

This is London 30/6/03

35

AN elderly heart patient was kicked off a bus in the rain for carrying a tin of paint.

Granddad Brian Heale, 73, who bought the antique cream emulsion for a DIY project, was told it broke new Health and Safety rules. The RAF veteran, who suffers from shortness of breath, found himself stranded because he could not carry the tin home. He took shelter in a café, whose owner gave him a lift home. Brian, who had caught the no. 9 bus in Cardiff, told how the driver ordered him: 'Sorry, you've got to get off.' He said: 'I thought he was joking. But he parked the bus and called head office. Then he told me carrying the paint was against new Health and Safety regulations. It's crazy.' Under the new rules paint is classed as a 'hazardous article' and can only be carried on buses if it is in a bag. A spokesman for Cardiff Bus said: 'We apologise to Mr Heale for the obvious inconvenience caused. Safety of passengers is our number one priority, which is why the company takes regulations very seriously.'

The Sun 18/4/06

Paddle guard puzzle
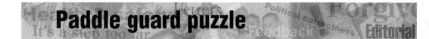

TOWN hall chiefs threatened to remove a kiddies' paddling pool – because it had no lifeguard. Katie Joyce and other mums chipped in for the 10 ft plastic pool to give their children a holiday treat. But when they set up the £50 inflatable on a council-owned communal green without permission, they were warned it would be removed on safety grounds. Bosses at Warwick District Council feared a child could get hurt, although the water was only 12 inches deep. They told families on the Fallow Hill estate in Leamington Spa not to let children use it. The letter added: 'Permission has not been granted for its use. The council cannot be held liable and persons using the pool are not insured. The council are considering removing it.' Residents say the council was unhappy because there was no lifeguard or first aider. But angry parents claim they watch the children and there are never more than six in the pool. Katie, 36, said: 'It's ridiculous, those kids could not be safer. The government always bangs on about getting children out of doors and here they are, in the open and entertained in a safe environment, yet we are told to stop.'

Daily Mirror 19/8/05

Post delivery scotched

A tiny coastal community is no longer receiving post after Royal Mail judged as too dangerous a footpath that postmen have walked along to reach it since Victorian times.

For more than 100 years a postman has walked the half-mile track to a cluster of crofts on the beautiful Ardmore peninsula on the northwest tip of Scotland. But Royal Mail now say that it has cancelled the service after a postman slipped and fell on a grassy slope, leading it to view the route as an 'unreasonable' risk to the health and safety of its workers. The journey, which takes about 30 minutes each way, includes heather-clad hills, lush woodland and a section of waterfall, and is safely navigated most days by a local mother and her two young children, aged 5 and 3. John Thurso, the Liberal Democrat MP for Caithness, Sutherland and Easter Ross, said that he believed the postman who fell had been denied the 'high-quality mountain boots' issued to those normally delivering to the area. A mountaineering adviser asked to assess the path concluded: 'This is a well-maintained footpath. It would be classified as an 'easy walk' on a national footpath grading system.'

The Times 7/7/06

Conker allergy nuts

PUPILS at two schools have been banned from playing conkers in case they suffer from a nut allergy. The head teachers feared children would suffer a nasty reaction just by touching them. But experts said the latest in a string of scares about kids playing conkers was simply bonkers. Head teacher Gary Postlethwaite acted after a number of parents of kids at Bookwell Primary School in Egremont, Cumbria, said they were worried about the danger. 'We have some children in school with severe nut allergies and children have been told not to bring conkers in.' But Sue Higgs, spokeswoman for the Anaphylaxis Campaign, which helps people with allergies, said: 'This seems an over-reaction. In all of our years of experience we have never come across anyone who has had a severe reaction to a conker.'

The Sun 7/10/04

Condom push blow

VOLUNTEER workers in the Lothians have been banned from issuing condoms to under-16s despite a rise in the number of teenage pregnancies. NHS Lothian ruled that only staff on the official payroll could hand out contraceptives and advice to under-16s.

It said restricting contact to 'suitably trained people' would ensure the safety and protection of children. Critics claimed hundreds of teenagers would be at risk of falling pregnant or catching sexually transmitted diseases. Dr Dean Marshall, deputy chairman of the BMA's Scottish GP committee, said the NHS was becoming 'risk averse'. He said: 'My concern is that child protection is used frequently as a reason for doing things.' The Family Planning Association in Scotland also condemned the decision. Director Tim Street said it was a 'great shame' that child protection issues were making it more difficult to put the message across to young people.

BBC News 22/5/06

Guard sacked for stopping suicide

A courageous hospital security guard has been sacked – for dramatically saving a patient from a suicide leap. Dad-of-three

39

Baid Tamoor, 34, climbed 15 ft up scaffolding as the man prepared to jump off after tying a noose around his neck. Without thought for his own safety, hero Baid grappled with the mentally ill patient and restrained him with the help of a paramedic. But instead of praising the guard, bosses fired him for breaking Health and Safety rules. Shocked Baid, who worked at Lewisham Hospital, South London, said: 'I can't believe it. Why should I leave my job for saving someone's life?'

After the scaffolding rescue, Baid, of Kidbrooke, South London, was given a dressing down and suspended from work. He was then sacked by his employers, First Management Group. In a statement with Lewisham Hospital, the security firm said Baid's actions were 'a serious breach of Health and Safety regulations'. A spokesman for First Management added: 'It may seem harsh and unfair. But our guards are employed to monitor security and report incidents to the police or fire service and not to risk their own safety.'

Suicide Reference Library 2/07

Crazy paving

A Police Community Support Officer has been banned from walking large swathes of her beat because of the lack of pavements in the rural area. Mrs Pooley complained she felt unsafe because of the risk of being hit by vehicles as she pounded the streets. Senior officers at Gloucestershire Police agreed she should not walk the beat for 'Health and Safety' reasons. Instead, she now makes her rounds by car through the narrow streets. The decision has been branded 'crazy' by incredulous villagers in the communities of South Cerney and Cerney Wick, near Cirencester, Gloucestershire. Parish

Council Clerk Maurice McKee asked: 'Do criminals need footpaths to carry out crimes? And if they don't, why do police need a footpath to patrol?' Pub landlord Martin Smith, who runs the Royal Oak in South Cerney, said: 'It's crazy. We're all up in arms about it. She should still be walking the streets. Why not – they have fluorescent jackets don't they?'

Daily Mail 21/10/06

Hat ban 'mad'

POLICE have banned Wimbledon's 'mad hatters' from bringing their props to the side of the famous tennis courts as part of a major security overhaul. Condemned by Tim Henman's fans as 'miserable' and 'killjoy', the move comes as new anti-terrorist measures are introduced at the tournament – including metal detectors, body searches of all spectators, and a bigger police presence. Even picnic hampers are banned. Superintendent Simon Ovens, in charge of security, said oversized hats that obscure people's views will be confiscated. 'We do not wish to spoil anyone's enjoyment but want to ensure a safe championship for all.' Pippa Robinson, 35, said: 'If Henman makes the semi-finals my husband would definitely want to be there with his Union flag hat on. He'll be really upset about this.' But Jean Tyson, who runs the Topspin Henman fan club, said: 'I'll be glad to see klaxons banned because they drive me absolutely nuts, and large hats and flags can be very annoying if you are sitting behind them. I think the authorities are just trying to calm things down a bit. The tournament has a unique atmosphere and we don't want it to become like the Barmy Army.'

Evening Standard 21/6/04

Pat ride purged

A Postman Pat kids' ride has been removed by officials who say it is a hazard. For six years youngsters have enjoyed the red van outside a shoe shop, but owner Sherryl Granger has been warned for not having a licence and posing a Health and Safety risk. She received a letter from precinct manager Shelley Filipi telling her to get rid of the ride at St Mary's Place, Market Harborough. Mrs Granger said: 'I have never known anything so petty. It's just a van that rocks up and down to the Postman Pat tune. Thousands of children have ridden on it. Even more people have walked by and we have never had a complaint.'

Derbygripe.co.uk 2/07

Quiet as a grave

WIND chimes have been banned from a cemetery because of complaints about the noise.

Hundreds of the chimes have been hung from trees by visiting mourners. Jeanette Monkley, who tends her grandparents' graves, said: 'It's lovely when the wind is blowing.' But council health and safety officials in Newport, Gwent, have ruled they must all be removed. John Davies, who visits his brother's grave, said: 'I thought it was a hoax.'

Daily Mirror 21/2/06

Tops dropped

PLASTIC spinning tops known as Beyblades have been banned from a prep school in Merseyside after a parent was reportedly injured by one. The toys have turned into a huge craze all over the country – three million have been sold in the UK already. Janet Skelly, head of Birkenhead Preparatory School, said Beyblades seemed like a good idea at first. She said they were popular with kids who didn't want to play football or basketball at break. But after hearing that a parent was hit in the eye by a top, Janet decided to ban them. She said: 'We've got to put the safety and wellbeing of the boys first.' The injuries apparently happen when the Beyblades are released in the air rather than on the ground as they are designed to be used.

BBC Newsround 14/2/03

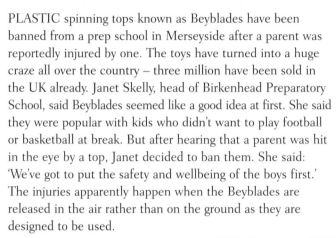

Head for heights

A European Union directive designed to promote safety on building sites must now be applied to rock climbers. Under the new rules, mountaineers may well endanger their lives by being obliged to fix two separate ropes to rock faces instead of the traditional one. The Heath and Safety Executive says it will also be necessary to fix safety notices on mountains to warn climbers when they are approaching icy or snow-covered surfaces. The move is said to have dismayed Britain's leading climbing and mountaineering organizations.

Daily Telegraph 17/8/03

Ski off Santa

SANTA has been banned from arriving at a harbour on water skis this Christmas because officials have deemed it unsafe. The appearance of the red-clad gentleman on water skis has proved a popular attraction at Wells in north Norfolk. But Wells harbourmaster Bob Smith confirmed the stunt had been ruled out on safety grounds and following complaints from last year's event. He said: 'We had complaints from other harbour users and, as much as we would have liked it to happen, we have to say no purely on safety grounds.'

Daily Mail 9/11/05

Dive ban bombs

A Cambridge teenager has launched a petition to force a rethink over a weekend diving ban at the city's Parkside Pools. 15-year-old Colin Boys, who has been diving during weekend public swimming sessions at the pool since he was seven, is devastated at the new rules. James Etherington, head diving coach, said: 'The diving board is a pretty dangerous piece of equipment and following various risk assessments we have decided to stop diving at times when the pool will be busy.' But Colin's father Laurence, said: 'I'd say it's loony-leftiness taken to crazy extremes.'

Cambridge Evening News 15/11/04

Sounding the alarm

VEHICLES used by Scots firefighters and police officers have been given extra soundproofing after tests showed siren noise could cause hearing damage to crews.

Grampian Fire and Rescue has spent £12 000 on sound-proofing its fire engines after Health and Safety experts found unacceptable levels of noise inside the cabs. Firefighters, who presumably think nothing of entering blazing buildings to save lives, were also advised to keep the windows closed to further reduce noise levels. And in Fife, the local police force has added soundproofing to its fleet of powerful BMW traffic cars and some riot vans in a bid to protect officers' hearing.

The Scotsman 12/8/06

Assembly ram ban

THE Welsh Assembly has been accused of discriminating against ruminants after a goat was banned from attending an official function. Shenkin, mascot of the Royal Regiment of Wales, had joined soldiers for a visit to the Assembly but caterers refused to serve a buffet until he was seen off the premises. An Assembly spokeswoman said: 'It was a Health and Safety matter and he had weed on the floor.' The Royal Windsor white goat, dressed in regimental colours, was making a second trip to the Cardiff Assembly. He had already met the Queen, the Prince of Wales and the Emperor of Japan. David Davies, the Conservative Assembly Member who had invited the regiment, demanded an apology for Shenkin, adding: 'Sinn Fein have been allowed to the Welsh Assembly, but not the mascot of one of Wales's finest and proudest fighting regiments. We went through all the correct security procedures … and as for weeing on the floor, I am sure he was just passing judgment on the record of the Assembly. Shenkin should receive an apology and be invited back for a special carrot sandwich,' he added.

The Times 14/2/03

OAP wire barb

A woman of 93 who put up barbed wire around her home after repeated burglaries has been ordered to take it down because it could injure intruders. Ruby Barber's family put up £450 worth of wire following three break-ins at her home in the Ryehill area of Northampton. But council officials have ordered them to take it down – because it could injure someone who 'foolishly' tries to climb it. Mrs Barber's son Burt told BBC Radio 4's Today programme: 'It's around the perimeter of the garden and along the back of the bungalow. That stops them totally. I can't see what else can be done unless they have a man standing guard there.' Without the barbed wire, he said, 'you are giving a Health and Safety charter to burglars to allow them to get in without a problem.'

BBC News 8/8/01

Hard hat Santa

A shopping centre Santa has been issued with a hard hat after local kids pelted him with mince pies. Mall boss Andrew MacKinnon says he is so worried about Santa's safety that he has now decided to make him wear specially designed protective headgear, complete with funky reindeer antlers. He said: 'We take the safety of our staff very seriously and have taken this somewhat drastic action to protect Santa from possible injury. Santa said: 'I don't want to let the children down so, even if it looks a bit odd, I will just have to wear my festive hard hat.' Mr MacKinnon added: 'I think this was a bit of Christmas high jinks by the local neds. I look on it as a Health and Safety matter more than anything else.' This is not the first time Santa has been targeted by bah-humbug neds at the Paisley Centre. Last year Mr MacKinnon said Father Christmas was set upon by a group of yobs, only to retaliate by picking up a Christmas tree from his grotto and setting about his attackers.

Paisley Daily Express 21/12/06

Finger-licking bad

HEALTH officials have warned Britain's TV chiefs to clean up their act. They claim the television cooks are flouting basic hygiene rules as they demonstrate their recipes. According to the Chartered Institute of Environmental Health, Jamie Oliver tends to spray saliva over ingredients as he speaks. He is also accused of licking his fingers and then dipping them into dishes. Nigella Lawson is criticised for keeping her rings on whilst cooking, which health experts say encourages bacteria to lurk. Other chefs, particularly on BBC2's Ready Steady Cook programme, have been singled out for failing to wash their hands. Another 'dangerous' practice is using the same chopping boards for raw meat and vegetables. Channel 4, which shows Nigella Bites, said Miss Lawson's passion for food was more important than perfect adherence to hygiene rules. A spokesman said: 'If we did exactly what should be done all viewers would see would be 30 minutes of Nigella washing her hands.'

This is London 27/12/02

Law jaw clamp

POLICE dogs are being muzzled to prevent them from biting criminals. Instead of clamping their jaws around the legs of suspects, the dogs are trained to leap at their targets and disable them with a flying butt. Senior officers claim that the new 'muzzle-strike' tactic is effective and has led to a reduction in injuries. The technique, pioneered in North Wales, may now be adopted by other forces. However, critics have accused the police of bowing to political correctness and human rights concerns. The policy follows a rise in compensation claims against forces from members of the public, and even serving officers, who have been bitten by police dogs. A critic of the tactic, John Barrett, a retired dog handler who served for 18 years with the Metropolitan Police, said: 'This sounds like political correctness. It is very strange. I think the public would laugh at you with a muzzled dog, and it could be counter-productive if people think the dog has to be muzzled because it is dangerous.'

Sunday Telegraph 15/10/06

Losing their marbles

A report by the Children's Society says many schools have banned marbles, handstands and skipping in case of accidents.

They also revealed that climbing trees was no longer allowed because pupils got their hands dirty. But psychologist Phillip Hodson says: 'Having a bloody knee after a game of tag is important to a child's development – as is learning by your own mistakes. It teaches you how to make decisions under pressure.'

Daily Mirror 28/2/05

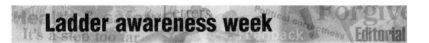

Ladder awareness week

GLOUCESTER Council is holding a meeting to warn people that ladders can be dangerous. The talk is part of National Ladders Week, during which officials will also make spot checks on businesses to raise 'ladder awareness'. The Council said: 'The most common causes of accidents include over-reaching, slipping from rungs, or the ladder falling. But Health and Safety officers are not considering a ban on ladders in the workplace.'

Derbygripe.co.uk 2/07

Santa hats binned

BINMEN have been banned from wearing Santa hats – on health grounds. The refuse collectors in Kingston upon Hull have worn the traditional red hats for years. Now City Council scrooges say 'it does not create a professional impression of the council'. A spokesman for the East Yorkshire city said: 'Employees can wear Christmas hats in their own time. Wearing them during work time does not create a professional impression. Further, there can be Health and Safety implications should hats get in the way of dangerous machinery operation.'

The Sun 9/12/06

Barmy bird ban

BIRDLOVERS Deborah and Graham Shearer can carry on feeding the birds in their garden after a council apology. The couple were warned by Health and Safety bosses not to give food to the feathered friends at their home in Simmondley, Glossop, after complaints. But High Peak Council now says it will review its procedures. Mrs Shearer, who has been feeding birds since she was a teenager, said: 'I'm just glad it's finally been sorted out.' Council chiefs said there had been complaints that the birds were noisy and that birdseed might attract rats.

Manchester Evening News 31/7/04

Don't eat the napkins

A bright idea to alert pensioners to the wiles of conmen and sneak thieves has been put on hold because of fears that some elderly clients might not only take the advice but eat it. Health and Safety rules were invoked to halt the distribution of free napkins printed with safety tips with meals-on-wheels in part of Gloucestershire after organisers were warned that there should have been a risk assessment of choking hazards. The hiccup left pensioners' leaders spluttering, if not choking themselves, at the instruction. Pat Scannell of Gloucestershire Pensioners' Forum said: 'To risk-assess a napkin is utterly ridiculous and an unnecessary cost to the taxpayer. People shouldn't think all pensioners are senile.' The napkins had already been printed with a simple slogan about not admitting strangers and details of the county's 'Lock, stop, chain and check' campaign for elderly or vulnerable people. But the delay has been sanctioned by the Crime and Disorder

Reduction Partnership in Tewkesbury, where the problem was raised at a meeting intended to give the final go-ahead. The group's development manager, Debbie Kemp, said: 'We were discussing it at the meeting and it was brought to our attention that we should consider Health and Safety issues.'

The Guardian 13/4/05

Palm crazy

PALM trees along the seafront at Torbay have been emblematic of the English Riviera for decades. Now they have become emblematic of the modern obsession with Health and Safety. Council officials have written to the Chamber of Trade saying the trees are a potential hazard because their sharp leaves could cause injuries to eyes or faces.

Daily Telegraph 10/6/06

HACK

Pulling the chain

A Catholic schoolgirl was asked not to wear a crucifix on a chain because it breached Health and Safety rules. Samantha Devine, 13, was told to remove the crucifix and chain to comply with school rules. She attends the Robert Napier School, a non-denominational mixed school, in Gillingham, Kent. Her father, Danny Devine, 30, of Canterbury Street, Gillingham, told the Medway Messenger: 'It's just political correctness gone absolutely mad. It's a harmless crucifix and she wears it as a symbol of her religion.' Deputy head teacher Paul Jackson defended the school's stance. He said: 'The school has a policy of no jewellery to be worn by any students in years seven to 10. All parents and students are aware of this. In this particular instance, the student, and parent, were informed that the wearing of the chain was a Health and Safety hazard, but that we would allow a lapel badge to be worn.'

The Sun 12/1/07

Down the plug

NEW rules mean that major electrical jobs in the kitchen and bathroom must be done by a qualified electrician. Householders who want to do it themselves will have to pay to get their work checked by council inspectors, which could be as expensive as getting in a professional. Building Regulations Minister Phil Hope insisted: 'This is all about saving lives and cutting injuries.' The Electrical Contractors Association said: 'It's a big step forward in raising the standard of electrical work in the home.' And charging for the privilege.

Derbygripe.co.uk 2/07

A shopkeeper has been ordered to remove his flags celebrating St George by council officials who say they breach Health and Safety rules. Phil Moffatt has been told the 20 flags hoisted from lampposts near his shop in Tuebrook, Liverpool, are dangerous.

But Mr Moffatt, who named his shop after Winston Churchill, vowed to defy the ban with the bulldog spirit. Mr Moffatt, who has flown the flags from the same lampposts for the last five years, was ordered to remove them or face a £1,000 bill from Liverpool City Council. 'It has really come to something when a proud Englishman can't raise a few flags to celebrate St George's Day,' he said. 'They have never caused any safety problems, and it seems to me that someone in the council is flexing their powers of political correctness.' But a council spokesman said: 'We are not trying to be spoilsports. There is a clear danger to Mr Moffatt himself and an obvious road safety hazard. The flags could distract drivers, fall off and hit cars or pedestrians, and it could encourage others to follow suit.'

BBC News 19/4/05

Nut ban nuts

MILLIONS of families are to miss out on a longstanding Christmas tradition following a decision by supermarkets not to stock Brazil nuts. The nuts, popular with afternoon tea around the Christmas tree, have been judged a potential safety risk by the European Commission. Traces of a toxin that can cause liver cancer have been found in their shells. So the EC has decreed every batch imported from Brazil must be tested for the substance aflatoxin. Supermarkets claim the cost of destroying any shipments would be too high and are not willing to import them. Brazil nut kernels, used in nut mixtures and chocolate Brazil nuts, can still be imported from Bolivia and Peru. But Peter Morgan of the Combined Edible Nut Trade Association said: 'Commercially it is now too risky to import them. The EU have put overly stringent limits on this without really good evidence.'

Evening Standard 3/12/04

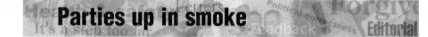

Parties up in smoke

A council has been labelled 'killjoys' and 'sad' after urging residents not to have family Guy Fawkes Night bonfires. It wants residents to put material they would have burned into garden composters instead. The Conservative-led Test Valley Council in Hampshire, which covers a mainly rural area around Andover and Romsey, advised its ratepayers to consider the environmental impact of having bonfires on November 5. It suggests attending an organised bonfire party as an alternative. 'Bonfires can cause annoyance to neighbours, and every year the council receives many complaints about bonfire nuisances,' it said. But Daniel Busk, a farmer and a member of the Council's executive, said he would be ignoring the advice and hoped to have it rescinded.

'This is typical of the nanny state taking all the fun out of life,' he said. 'This is an absolute joke: bloody stupid, ridiculous. It is much better to burn your leaves in the garden than drive your car somewhere using petrol.'

Daily Telegraph 22/10/05

Ig in outing ban

A shopping centre has closed the doors on a 4 ft long lizard, which was the regular companion of a Tyneside man. Bosses at Gateshead's Metrocentre told Paul Hudson, 26, that Health and Safety concerns prevented him walking his pet iguana, called Ig. Mr Hudson, from Gateshead, said he had taken Ig into the complex since 1998. 'He is a nice animal. He could bite someone if he wanted to but he wouldn't. It's not in him, he's well looked after and likes his days out.' But officials at the shopping complex said they had to put the concerns of customers first. A spokeswoman for the Metrocentre said: 'We have to stick by our rules otherwise we would have to allow other people to bring their cats, dogs, hedgehogs or budgies with them. I am sorry, but the answer on this occasion is that we have to look after our customers first and have to say no to the iguana.'

BBC News 25/9/06

Too cool for cats

SCENES that appear to glamorise smoking are to be edited out of Tom and Jerry cartoons following complaints to Ofcom, the broadcasting watchdog, because they are not appropriate to be shown to children. The complaint was about two cartoons – Texas Tom and Tennis Chumps – transmitted on Turner Broadcasting's children's channel, Boomerang. More than half (56%) of the channel's audience are aged four to 14.

In Texas Tom, Tom tries to impress a female cat by making a rollup cigarette, while Tennis Chumps sees Tom's opponent in

55

a match smoking a large cigar. Turner said it would edit out any references in Tom and Jerry and all its 1700 Hanna Barbera cartoons in which smoking appeared to be condoned. But the broadcaster said editing out all smoking references might adversely affect the 'value of the animation'. Ofcom welcomed Turner's approach but said in future it would look at all such cases individually.

The Guardian 22/8/06

Bad vibrations

BRITAIN'S defence chiefs are fighting to prevent the army's tanks being stopped in their tracks by the introduction of a European directive on vibration and noise at work. The Control of Vibration at Work Regulations and the Control of Noise at Work Regulations have left officers scrambling to discover if the military's armoured vehicles break the rules. 'If you are in a combat situation then clearly it will be difficult to bring in these regulations,' explained a spokesman for the Health and Safety Executive.

Daily Telegraph 2/9/05

Egg box mix-up

EGG boxes are to return to craft lessons at an East Sussex school after they were banned over health fears. The head of Wallands Primary School in Lewes said he had been enforcing the ban, believing the reason was a risk of spreading salmonella. After meeting county council chiefs, he said he would soon be able to let pupils use the egg boxes again. But East Sussex

County Council said it had never banned the materials at any school and there had been a mix-up. Brian Davies, head teacher at the school, said he had been stopping pupils bringing in egg boxes or used toilet rolls for several years.

He said he was told they were unsafe by the council and thought it was due to fears that salmonella could be spread to the schoolchildren. Mr Davies said: 'It's the sort of thing we get the whole time these days.'

BBC News 21/6/05

Council grabs conkers

CHILDREN are now being denied the autumnal pleasure of collecting conkers as council workers will be there ahead of them in the supposed interests of Health and Safety.

Rather than risk children damaging themselves or property by collecting the horse chestnuts, Newcastle Upon Tyne City Council is responding to residents' requests to get to them first. Taxpayers are funding the operation by the council's environmental services team to use a cherry picker crane to strip trees bare of conkers before children can get their hands on them. But members of the public have been stunned by the sight of the conker-picking team at work. Martin Callanan, the northeast's Tory MEP, said: 'Words fail me. It's the nanny state gone mad. I used to collect conkers as a lad and I never injured myself and nor did any of my friends. There must be better things they could do with their time. They could clean the streets for a start.'

Evening Standard 10/10/06

Meltdown for Mr Whippy

FOR 60 years the tinny jingle of Greensleeves that announced the arrival of the ice-cream van has been an indelible memory of childhood, but that sound may soon be removed from suburban streets. Health lobbyists have decided that ice-creams are too much of a danger to children's health. MPs and health officials are planning a series of measures across the country that are already forcing Mr Whippy and his helpers into meltdown.

Under an amendment to the Education and Inspection Bill, local authorities will be given new powers to stop ice-cream vans from operating near school gates. The move comes as operators claim that they are already being forced out of business by an over-zealous health lobby. Greenwich Council, in south-east London, has banned the vans from its streets altogether, while in Scotland, West Dunbartonshire Council has introduced an exclusion zone around schools for vans. Mark Gossage, the director of Ice Cream Alliance, which represented 20 000 van owners in the 1960s and now has 700 members, said that many of his members can no longer make a living. 'Many schools have already stopped arrangements for vans to sell to pupils,' he said. 'They are wiping us out.'

The Times 8/5/06

Smoke out granny

NURSING home staff have told patient Gladys Gornall to go outside if she wants a cigarette – even though she's 93. But wheelchair-bound Gladys, who only began smoking ten years ago when she was widowed, fumed: 'I'll catch my death out there. I should at least be allowed to have a fag in my own room – I am an adult, after all.' Bosses said the indoor smoking ban at Norwood Lodge in Portishead, Somerset, was a Health and Safety issue.

The People 22/6/06

Party parts pooper

THE perils of holding a Christmas party have been spelt out by safety campaigners, urging firms to make sure their staff do not injure themselves by dancing on desks or photocopying parts of their body. Similarly, managers have been advised not to put up any mistletoe, in case it leads to complaints of sexual harassment. The Royal Society for the Prevention of Accidents and the TUC have published a special checklist, saying that while they weren't being 'party poopers' they wanted to lessen the chances of workers ending up in hospital after a festive bash. They warn that candles, flaming puddings and smoking should all be banned at Christmas parties. Stepladders should be used to put up decorations, as using a swivel chair could cause an accident. And workers should resist the temptation to photocopy parts of their body, because of the risk of glass in painful places if the machine breaks.

Mail on Sunday 10/12/04

Big Ted ban

ENORMOUS teddies given as prizes in gambling arcades are facing extinction after being labelled too much of a temptation. Ministers fear the huge cuddly toys are so appealing they could lure youngsters into a lifetime of gambling. They say the furry animals must be downsized to reduce the risk. But the plans have been ridiculed by opposition politicians, who are accusing the government of running a nanny state.

The Department of Culture, Media and Sport argues that young people should still be allowed to play at the arcades but believes the prizes should not be too big. A spokesman said: 'The government believes that children should be able to play these machines but the stakes and prizes should discourage them playing too much.'

This is London 26/1/05

Desperate safety measure

ONE of the UK's most popular comics has been taken off the shelves at a leading airport as part of a security crackdown. Security staff have ordered copies of the Dandy – made famous by cowboy Desperate Dan – to be withdrawn from Birmingham International Airport because a free toy gun is being given away. The bright blue-and-yellow plastic 'punch-gun' toy was attached to hundreds of copies of the comic, and the airport fear it could be used as a weapon to hijack a plane. But the Dandy's publishers branded the decision 'a hysterical over-reaction' after security officers said the cheap plastic toy was not suitable for sale within the airport terminal. A spokesman for DC Thomson said: 'It's obviously a toy and nothing more. It might be mildly irritating if a kid fired it at your head over and over, but it's hardly a weapon of mass destruction. I don't think a terrorist would get very far if he tried to hijack a plane with a free toy from the Dandy. I know they have to be strict about security at airports, but this ruling is just ridiculous. It's a hysterical over-reaction.'

Birmingham Post 28/2/03

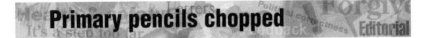

Primary pencils chopped

A school has banned children from taking pencil cases into class in case they are used to hide sharp weapons. St Anne's Primary School in Denton, Greater Manchester, acted after a boy was cut with a letter opener. Nick Seaton, chairman of the Campaign for Real Education, said: 'Most parents will think it is ridiculous to ban pencil cases just because one child carries a letter opener in his. It seems a bit extreme. Serious action should be taken against the particular individual, but to ban pencil cases universally is silly.'

Derbygripe.co.uk 2/07

THE seaside town of Scarborough has cancelled plans to switch on its Christmas lights after fears of a compensation claim if anyone was injured. The problems began when North Yorkshire Fire Service claimed the town centre could cope with only 2000 visitors. The decision has outraged residents, who condemned it as yet another intrusion of the 'nanny state'. Penny Marsden, an independent councillor and shop-keeper, said the whole thing was 'a joke'. She said: 'It is another result of the ill-thought-out regulations imposed by the government. This is a joyous occasion when children come out to enjoy the start of Christmas – and we are going to rob them of it.' Town centre manager Malcolm Hall said he had tried to obtain anti-surge barriers and stewards, but had failed. 'We're all bitterly disappointed, but the health and safety of people is paramount,' he added.

Evening Standard 13/11/06

School missile alert

PUPILS have been banned from throwing paper planes to one another – in case they get injured. Staff at a Kent primary school have instead set up special targets in the playground for the children to aim at. The edict follows claims by teachers that a few of the school's pupils, aged between three and 11, had been 'over-zealous' in launching the missiles. The head teacher argued the ban was 'a sensible' measure – but parents of some of the 230 pupils reacted with disbelief. One father of a seven-year-old boy said: 'I've heard it all now. We made paper planes and our parents did the same and I never heard of anyone getting hurt. It's taking the Health and Safety measures to absurd lengths. Heaven knows what they will think to ban next.' Staff at Bishops Down Primary School in Tunbridge Wells, Kent, introduced the ban after two pupils were seen aiming their paper planes at other children. Head teacher Emma Savage said staff were particularly concerned about eye injuries. 'These planes can have sharp edges and have the potential to damage a young person's eyes,' she said.

Daily Mail 18/6/06

OAP explosion fear

A sick pensioner who relies on an oxygen cylinder to breathe has been banned from her local club – because she's a fire hazard. Smoker Gillian Western, 66, has been barred from the

Royal British Legion in case her life-saving cylinder explodes. Wheelchair-user Gillian, who suffers from chronic bronchial asthma, said: 'I have been a member for more than 25 years and have been going in there with the cylinder for two years. I think they are just being petty.' Jeff Harrison of the Royal British Legion in Cheshire said it was the committee's decision on how they run the club. 'There is a Health and Safety difficulty because of smoking. Therefore they have asked her to keep out. It's as simple as that.'

The Sun 16/12/04

Jellies stamped out

JELLY mini-cup sweets have been banned by a European directive because of a risk of children choking. The sweets are packaged in plastic cups and designed to be swallowed in one. The European Commission said they were a risk because of their 'consistency, shape and form', and that warnings alone were not enough to protect children. But opponents said the ban was disproportionate and there was no evidence of a danger to children's health. The jelly sweets contain additives derived from seaweed or certain gums. They are individual, mouth-sized servings and may contain a small piece of preserved fruit, including apple and mango. They are designed to be projected into the mouth by exerting pressure on the semi-rigid container and then eaten in one single bite. However, Tory MEP John Bowis, Conservative health spokesman in the European Parliament, said: 'This decision by the commission is completely over the top and disproportionate.'

BBC News 3/4/04

Plane crazy

A family was dumped off a plane because 'Jobsworth' cabin crew wouldn't let a three-month-old baby sit on a kind-hearted passenger's knee in case he was abused. When Ann Jordan was told she couldn't fly because she had the wrong safety seat for daughter Azrael, another passenger offered to look after baby Kaleb so the family could stay on board. But the captain refused and ordered the family off, citing 'child protection laws'. Angry mum-of-two Ann, 35, of Rutherglen Road, Red House, Sunderland, said: 'It was insulting, not just to me but to the passenger who wanted to help.' Low-budget airline EasyJet defended its pilot, saying he was complying with policy. It also says the crew was right not to compromise passengers' safety. Housewife Ann was flying from Bristol to Newcastle, after visiting family in Cardiff. She was marched off the plane in tears as concerned passengers tried to negotiate with staff. Ann said: 'He could easily have allowed the baby to sit next to me on the kind lady's knee where I could keep a close eye, but he was too much of a jobsworth.'

Sunderland Echo 13/2/07

Put out no flags

FLYING flags from the MPs' office building near the House of Commons has been banned – because it's too dangerous. Health and Safety experts say it is unsafe for workers to put up flags on the flagpole at Portcullis House. Flag raisers have to climb over ventilation ducts in poor light, without a safety harness. It means a flag has been flown only once since the problem-plagued building for MPs and their staffs opened in

2000. Labour MP John Spellar said: 'This is a case of bungling bureaucrats and architects not thinking things through.'

Sunday Mirror 28/1/07

One snack too many

A boy aged ten has been banned from his school dining hall because his packed lunch broke the government's healthy eating guidelines. The father of Ryan Stupples is protesting after his son was forced to eat in the headmaster's office at Lunsford Primary School, Larkfield, Kent, because his lunch contained two snacks, instead of one.

Ryan's lunch consisted of a sandwich, fruit, fromage frais, cake, mini cheese biscuits and a bottle of water. The cake and the biscuits broke the snack limit. They were discovered when a teacher checked his lunch box. The boy's father, Michael Stupples, 41, said: 'What 10-year-old boy won't get upset when he's thrown out of a dining hall in front of everyone and made to eat his lunch in the head teacher's office?' Malcolm Goddard, the headmaster, said: 'We take healthy eating very seriously and everyone is aware of our new policies.'

Daily Telegraph 14/10/06

Don't rung the police

POLICE called in to investigate vandalism at a mediaeval church refused to inspect the damage because, they told church officials, they didn't have specialist 'ladder training'.

Two gently leaning 12 ft ladders led to the five broken windows, some of which date from the 14th century. But the officers decided it was too dangerous to go up and take photographs. Now the churchwarden has criticised safety rules which he claims work in the criminals' favour. David Brennan, 57, said: 'Pretty soon police are going to be told not to chase burglars and muggers. Police forces are becoming increasingly powerless and unable to do the job because of ridiculous safety laws.' The windows were smashed at Middleton Parish Church, near Rochdale, causing £10 000 of damage.

Daily Mail 11/3/05

Pub bans glasses

A girl of six was left in tears after being barred from a pub playground – for wearing glasses. Lauren Brown was told it was a safety issue. But her mum Sarah said Lauren couldn't see without her specs. Angry Sarah added: 'She was so upset.' The Cherry Orchard pub in Woodchurch, Wirral, has apologised.

The People 5/3/06

Ambulance weighting

HEAVY patients could be banned from riding in emergency ambulances in the Bristol area. The public service workers' union Unison has warned ambulance crews they risk breaking the law by exceeding vehicle weight limits. Union leaders are raising the prospect of a ban on anyone over 18 st 8 lbs (260 lb) travelling in an emergency vehicle in the Avon Ambulance Trust area. The bid to enforce the strict limits could also mean patients are forced to travel without accompanying relatives, and midwives may be banned from travelling with pregnant women.

Police in bus fear

A police force has been criticised for not allowing a Community Support Officer to catch a bus to his beat on Health and Safety grounds. Ian Yeomans was supposed to cover the Gloucestershire village of South Cerney from a police station three miles away, but the job did not come with a car. The parish council suggested Mr Yeomans used the hourly bus services. But Gloucestershire police said he would not be allowed to until the Health and Safety implications had been examined. Mike Stuart, council chairman, said: 'This over-cautious attitude has really gone beyond the realms of reality.' Inspector Steve Williams said a Health and Safety check was needed for 'all police activity'. The saga looks as if it will have a happy ending without Mr Yeomans having to risk the bus – Gloucestershire police are going to pay for him to have access to a car.

The Guardian 29/4/06

OAP abuse worry

ROTARIANS, the pillars of local respectability, have been told they can no longer carry out charitable work with the old or the young while alone. The club, whose motto is Service Above Self, has decreed members must be accompanied when helping children or pensioners in case they are accused of abusing them. In a decision which has outraged many of the 58 000 British and Irish Rotarians, the Club Board has issued the instructions to local groups after being told insurance premiums against legal action would be 'sky high' if they did not follow the pairing system. A Rotary Club spokesman said the organisation had reluctantly introduced the measures after receiving legal advice. 'It is a case of having a witness present at all times, as a response to the nanny state we live in,' he said.

This is London 4/11/06

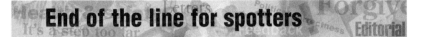

End of the line for spotters

HORDES of angry train-spotters are letting off steam over news that their number could soon be up. Security and safety issues have led to fears that rail companies will ban the UK's 100 000 spotters from stations. A report in Railway Magazine highlighted a number of worrying platform problems. One man was told to leave Britain's biggest interchange, Clapham Junction in South London, because he was 'breaching security'. Railway Magazine editor Nick Pigott said: 'The authorities are picking on a harmless hobby that has never caused a problem. It is a total breach of civil liberties.' Colin Smith, 52, from Bermondsey, southeast London, said: 'Sod 'em all. I've been doing this since I was six and nobody's going to stop me.'

The Sun 30/5/03

Walk training

FIRE bosses have defended a decision to stop firefighters from running during on-duty training sessions. Merseyside

Fire Service issued the ban after being sued by a firefighter who slipped during an exercise session and tore his knee ligaments. Gavin Bassie was awarded £100 000 in compensation after the accident, which ended his 13-year career.

The ban, which the Fire Service said was temporary, was branded 'ludicrous' by the Fire Brigades Union.

BBC News 13/12/05

Wimbledon flop

PATRIOTIC tennis fans have been banned from waving national flags at Wimbledon – because of fears over Health and Safety. Wimbledon authorities confiscated scores of England flags from fans watching Tim Henman's opening match at the tennis championship. They said they were removing all flags larger than 2 ft by 2 ft for 'Health and Safety' reasons, claiming the flags' poles could be dangerous. Matt Pateman, 23, from Bedfordshire, was using his 3 ft by 2 ft St George's Cross flag as a mat to sit on, but was told to put it in his bag or risk confiscation. He said: 'I couldn't believe it. I wasn't even waving it around – I was only sitting on it.' Paul Lewis, 28, a business manager from Chiswick, West London, said: 'There is no way that I was a danger to anybody. I wasn't even waving my flag: I was just holding it in my hands. It's ridiculous that they think having a flag is dangerous.' A spokesman for the All England Lawn Tennis Club said: 'The poles could cause injury to those sitting around.'

Daily Mail 27/6/06

No to Yo-ball

THE government has banned a controversial new toy, the Yo-ball – the first ban on a toy for more than a decade. Trading standards officers across the country have been warning of the dangers of the toys, fluid-filled brightly coloured plastic balls on rubber strings. The officers said there was a risk that children could be strangled if the string became wrapped around their necks, because it constricts. A spokesman for the Department of Trade and Industry said: 'The supply of Yo-balls is banned with immediate effect after tests have shown that the toy could pose a risk of strangulation.'

Evening Standard 24/4/03

No flowers

GRIEVING families have been banned from planting flowers at death crash scenes – because they're a safety hazard. Mini-gardens built as tributes to victims will be dug up and wreaths allowed at a site for only 30 days, warns Thurrock Council, Essex. It said: 'We respect the need for people to grieve. But others are putting their lives at risk to place flowers or visit permanent tributes.' But one angry dad said: 'It's nonsense and disrespectful.'

The People 20/8/06

BLACKPOOL'S landau horses will not be wearing nappies in time for the start of this holiday season. The future of the dung-catching devices has been thrown into doubt after councillors were told they could pose a serious Health and Safety threat. David Muir, equine consultant to the RSPCA, told a council meeting: 'What if the horse panics, puts its leg back, gets caught in the device and three people end up dead? We have to do a lot more research into the pros and cons of these devices before we put them on horses.' The delay in making horses wear nappies has come as a blow to Town Hall bosses, who hoped their introduction would put an end to the smelly problem of horse muck on the Promenade. Horse vet Barry Johnson said: 'Any piece of equipment added to a horse carries extra risks, and the nappy is no exception.' If the nappies are deemed too dangerous to wear, the future of the traditional Blackpool landau will be thrown into doubt.

Blackpool Gazette 10/2/07

IS this a dagger I see before me? Or is it 'an object which is designed for the purpose of inflicting bodily harm' and therefore unfit for the British stage? According to new guidelines published by the Health and Safety Executive, Macbeth would do well to consult a qualified armourer and slip into some protective clothing before conjuring up a potentially dangerous sharpened object in the corridors of Dunsinane. The guidance sets out to enlighten thespians on the 'management' of props in theatre, film and television. In a section entitled 'Noise', the executive stumbles upon the truth that 'firearms can produce very high levels' of it. On page five, the document states that 'it is worth noting that wood, plastic or rubber weapons may be hazardous if used in a stabbing or lunging mode'. It also adds that standing in front of a loaded crossbow may carry serious health implications. Members of the entertainment industry are bewildered. Malcolm Ranson, a fight choreographer who specialises in period sword play, said that the recommendations – including the revelation that performers' shoes 'should fit correctly'– were obvious. 'Most people would look at this and say it's all common sense,' he said. 'You sometimes wonder who it's actually aimed at.' The Management of Firearms and Other Weapons in Productions is one of 20 information pamphlets released in connection with the entertainment industry.

The Times 27/10/03

Church kites grounded

ROSSENDALE Council has grounded a fundraising kite contest organised by a local church. The event was to be held to mark the fall of the Taliban in Afghanistan, where kite flying has also been banned. The council said accident and damage insurance documents had not been completed. As the church was planning to charge an entry fee and the event was to be staged on council land, they could not grant permission. The

Rev. Ron Phillips of Sion Baptist Church, who organized the event, said: 'We could not help but make the comparison between what the Taliban did and this. It seems surprising that you need permission for something as simple and harmless as kite-flying. It was disappointing, but I understand the concerns of Rossendale Council.' Owen Williams, the council's chief executive, said: 'Any event which charges people to participate has to be covered by public liability insurance. It does not matter what activity is taking place. Public liability is even needed for bouncy castles.'

Manchester Evening News 14/10/04

Kids can't crab

THE traditional seaside pastime of collecting crabs from rock pools is to be banned in Suffolk because of fears over Health and Safety. Felixstowe Ferry has been a popular crabbing place for children, but now Suffolk County Council is changing warning signs to prevent the hobby. It says youngsters could easily slip and fall on the wet jetty where the Deben Ferry docks. The council says the new signs are to reinforce a ban already in place. It says crabbing has never been allowed at the jetty, despite people using it for decades. The British Crabbing Championships are held every year along the Suffolk coast at Walberswick.

BBC News 15/4/05

Riding takes a fall

BRITAIN'S love affair with horse riding is coming under increasing threat from the growing compensation culture.

According to the British Horse Society, dozens of pony trekking centres and riding schools are being forced to close because of spiralling insurance costs and customer claims. Some riding schools have seen insurance costs increase fivefold in the past five years. Chris Doran, a spokesman for the BHS, said the blame culture had caused 'big problems' for the business. She added: 'There was a time when someone who fell off would dust themselves down and get back on again. Not any more.' The crisis has seen the number of riding schools in the UK fall from 2500 to 1900 in recent years, and dozens of pony trekking centres in England have been forced to close. Malcolm Tarling, of the Association of British Insurers, said: 'Horses are inherently dangerous and injuries can be serious.'

Daily Telegraph 14/7/04

High risk Xmas

OFFICE workers at Tower Hamlets Council have been banned from hanging up Christmas decorations at work in case they get hurt. Staff who have just moved into a newly opened office building next to the Town Hall were barred via email from climbing to the ceiling to put up paper decorations in case they injured themselves and then sued the council. Fairy lights have also been banned in a bid to cut power bills and ensure safety standards. Mini Christmas trees, tinsel and baubles are still allowed – provided there are no lights. The council insisted it had not cancelled Christmas, however, saying it intended only to warn staff not to climb on to desks to put up decorations for fear they might fall. Staff could still celebrate Christmas with tinsel, baubles, and other decorations, the council said.

Daily Mail 23/11/06

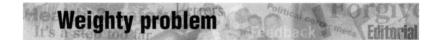

Building cover-up

THE government will decide whether or not UK builders will be banned from working bare-chested after MEPs voted to pass the buck. The European Commission's controversial Optical Radiation Directive was designed to protect workers exposed to X-rays or welding equipment. But an attempt to extend the EU legislation to cover 'natural' radiation – sunlight – was watered down after claims that Britain's construction workers would be forced to cover up at work. Conservative MEP Philip Bushill-Matthews said the tan-ban idea was 'barmy', adding: 'This raised the prospect of fully clothed life-guards in open-air swimming pools.'

The Sun 7/9/05

Weighty problem

A group of flower enthusiasts has been hit with a ban on hanging baskets after fears that they posed a public risk. For almost two decades hanging baskets have been a part of Bury St Edmunds' summer floral displays. But this year they will be absent from the Suffolk town after the council ruled there was a risk they could fall from lamp posts and injure the public. The council felt the town's lamp posts could not cope with the added weight of the pots of soil and could break. Michael Ames, chairman of the Bury in Bloom committee, said the ban by Suffolk County Council was pointless. 'They are guarding their own backs over health and safety,' he said. 'But no-one has been hurt – certainly not in Bury St Edmunds, certainly not in Suffolk.' Guy Smith, assistant highways manager for the council, said they just wanted to ensure the safety of

the public as some baskets were quite heavy. The council felt
they could present a safety hazard on some of the older lamp
posts. 'We have to be satisfied that the columns are strong
and stable enough to take the weight,' he said.

BBC News 10/2/04

World Cup willies

MOTORISTS who attach England flags to their car windows
ahead of the World Cup may wish to reconsider. According to
police in Hampshire, dangerously executed displays of patriotism
can scare wildlife, cause horses to bolt, and may result in
criminal prosecution. Officers at the force's wildlife crime
office warn that the 'loud flutter' generated by car window
flags was startling horses and other wildlife, particularly in the
New Forest area. They also stressed that if flags became
detached from vehicles they could turn into 'plastic missiles
hurtling though the air', which could cause serious injury.
Mark Perryman of the England fans supporters' club said: 'If
there is a serious Health and Safety issue it needs to be taken
seriously. But I was at Old Trafford for England's last match
and about 25% of the cars carried flags. I didn't see any of
them flying off and blinding people.'

The Guardian 1/6/06

Mountain scaffolders

THEY are perhaps the summit of Brussels-inspired lunacy: a
series of bizarre new safety regulations that have stirred up
something of a blizzard among British climbers.

Under new guidelines, climbers will have to swap ropes for scaffolding and mountain paths will feature signs warning that 'Snow is slippery'. Walkers will have to conduct 'risk assessments' and working in 'unfavourable weather conditions' is discouraged. Instructors will also be prevented from teaching groups on their own. 'This is the nanny state gone mad,' said mountaineer Sir Chris Bonington of the Outward Bound organisation. 'The whole point of the outdoor industry is that there is an element of risk. It is all about learning how to manage that,' he said. 'Without that, we might as well pack up.'

This is London 26/3/04

Police wrapped over wrists

A police force has banned officers from wearing charity wristbands – for Health and Safety reasons. Bobbies are bemused by the ban because they regularly wear watches, copper rheumatism bracelets and Remembrance Day poppies while on duty. Supt Peter Nicholson confirmed that all officers had been 'reminded' that the West Yorkshire Police dress code strongly deters them from sporting the wristbands. Millions of people wear the colourful bands to support campaigns such the fight on racism and bullying. Even Tony Blair wore one to help combat poverty in Africa. Michael Downes, of the West Yorkshire Police Federation, said: 'If a manager was concerned for officers' safety, we would support that. But if it was because they don't like these bands, we would be opposed to that.'

Daily Mirror 13/6/05

Time called on tea

COUNCIL bosses have slapped a ban on kind-hearted wardens who make tea for Birmingham's pensioners – because they say it's too dangerous. The ruling, which will cover all of the city's sheltered housing schemes, was blasted as 'red tape gone mad' by parched residents. Also off the menu are the cooked break-fasts they used to enjoy for £1 each in the communal area. The cooker has been removed because it's too hazardous. Health and Safety chiefs have ordered a ban on wardens brewing up in case one of the 61 residents gets scalded. 'The whole warden system has been completely dehumanised. It's not the fault of the wardens, it's the system,' said Jim Nicholl, vice chairman of the City Housing Liaison Board. A City Council spokesman said: 'Sheltered housing is about promoting independent living, and it's never been the role of wardens to make tea and coffee.' But disabled great-grandfather Mick Dodd, who lives in a bungalow with his wife Gill, said: 'We have a warden nearby who pops her head round the door about three times a week, but she's not allowed to make us a cup of tea.'

Birmingham Evening Mail 10/5/04

Gravel voice

AUCTIONEER David Probert has been told to keep his voice down – because it poses a risk to Health and Safety. Council officials have launched an investigation into Mr Probert's voice and demanded that he prove he does not make excessive noise. But the 59-year-old grandfather has understandably dismissed the inquiry as 'Health and Safety gone mad'. Mr Probert, who has received several letters from Worcester Health and Safety Executive, said: 'I have been a respected auctioneer for 40 years and have never heard of anything so ridiculous.'

Daily Mail 29/6/06

Not to be taken internally

FOUNTAIN pens are too dangerous for children under the age of 14, the British Standards Institution says. After decades when young pupils were encouraged to master penmanship, the benefits of developing good handwriting are now seen to be outweighed by the risk of swallowing the cap. Pen-maker Waterman has inserted a small slip with its pens which reads: 'This product is not intended for use by anyone under the age of 14 years.' British Standard 7272 sets out strict guidelines on how pens should be made.

It says a pen cap should have a small hole to allow a child to breathe if he or she swallows it. 'This has the effect of law,' said Dave Ruderman, of Waterman. Some adult pens are now defined as jewellery and therefore fall outside BS 7272. Mary Noble, a calligrapher, said: 'It is bad enough that children are learning to type on a computer rather than proper handwriting. When they do write, they use ballpoints and rolling balls. Children should not have to wait until they are 14.' Simon Gray, of the Battersea Pen Home, a specialist dealer, was appalled. He said: 'This is a bit like those bags of nuts which have labels saying "this bag contains nuts".' Kevin Jones, the headmaster of St John's College School, Cambridge, with 460 pupils aged four to 13, said: 'Perhaps I will have to employ pen police.'

Daily Telegraph 23/11/05

CHILDREN have been banned from playing tag in their village school playground after their headmistress branded the centuries-old game, along with others that involve physical contact, as 'inappropriate behaviour'. Youngsters aged five to 11 at Bracebridge Heath Primary School near Lincoln have been told there will be no kiss-chase, and even linking arms with each other will not be allowed. The only time any of the 400 pupils can touch each other is if they need to help a classmate who has fallen over. Mrs Tuck became concerned that play-ground games were becoming too rough after a number of instances of bumped heads. But parents at the school appeared more bemused than supportive over the ban. One said: 'I can't say I'm happy with it. I can't see it does much for children learning to play together.' Liz Carnell, of the charity Bullying Online, said: 'Parents these days are very quick to complain if a child does get hurt at school, so maybe the school is just trying to cover this eventuality. But I don't think this will stop bullying as it will never stop name-calling. Supervised games with an older child or a teacher watching are perhaps the answer.'

Evening Standard 9/2/07

HACK

Goggle boy ban

A ten-year-old boy who went swimming at Moorways Leisure Centre, Allenton, was told he could not practise while wearing a plastic snorkel mask because it was a danger to other swimmers. But he would have been fine wearing plastic goggles. Theresa Knight, spokeswoman for Derby City Council, said: 'Snorkel masks are banned at swimming pools across the city in case the glass or plastic in them smashes.' She added: 'We would have to clear the pool, drain it and then clean it, which would inconvenience a lot of people. We have no signs up indicating which items are banned because we would rather educate people ourselves if we see them taking something into the pool that is not allowed. We're not planning to put signs up, but it is something we may look into.'

Derbygripe.co.uk 2/07

Hugs off

A school headmaster was branded a killjoy after he ordered pupils to stop hugging each other. Steven Kenning told teens to quit embracing because it made them late for lessons. He said hugging could be deemed 'inappropriate' and 'victims' could be hugged against their will. The barmy 'safety' rule was posted on the website of Callington Community College, Cornwall. Mr Kenning said: 'Hugging was happening extensively and becoming the norm. We were worried it might become inappropriate. So we nipped it in the bud.' He added that there had been complaints from some pupils, so he told the kids: 'This is very serious not only for the victim but for anyone accused of acting inappropriately.' But the ban outraged parents and pupils at the 1250-pupil college, with some claiming they had been punished for illegal hugs. Local councillor Kath Pascoe said: 'I don't see anything wrong with hugging – it's better than fighting.'

The Sun 4/11/06

Costly bag study

THE government has come up with a study into the problem of opening plastic bags – at a mere £100 000 cost to taxpayers – all in the name of safety. A team of leading consultants and academics was appointed to research how volunteers coped with opening cereal bags, packets of cheese, cartons of orange juice and toilet freshener containers. And in an 86-page document they reported vital findings such as: 'The larger the area for grasping the more force can be applied to open a package.' MPs were less than impressed that taxpayers had to cough up for the research, carried out for Trade Secretary Patricia Hewitt's department. Liberal Democrat Mark Oaten said: 'It is the nanny state gone mad. Next they'll be telling us how to wipe our bottoms.' And Shadow Trade Secretary Tim Yeo added: 'This is an astonishing way to spend taxpayers' money. The busybodies in Whitehall are just finding things to do.' But the Department of Trade and Industry insisted that the study was serious and was carried out to improve safety. A spokesman added: 'This is valuable, important work. There are many people who have difficulties opening modern packaging. There are injuries caused because those who can't open packets use knives and scissors instead.'

Daily Mirror 18/1/03

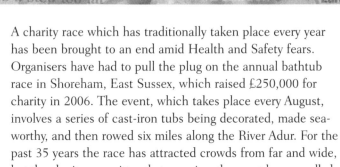

A charity race which has traditionally taken place every year
has been brought to an end amid Health and Safety fears.
Organisers have had to pull the plug on the annual bathtub
race in Shoreham, East Sussex, which raised £250,000 for
charity in 2006. The event, which takes place every August,
involves a series of cast-iron tubs being decorated, made sea-
worthy, and then rowed six miles along the River Adur. For the
past 35 years the race has attracted crowds from far and wide,
but the charity committee that organises the event has cancelled
it due to concerns over Health and Safety. Bath Tub Race
Committee Chairman Tony Jelliman said: 'It's a wacky race
which has generally been great fun, but increasing Health and
Safety requirements, insurance rates and other problems mean
that this kind of activity is no longer viable. It's unfortunate, but
that's the way the world is moving these days.'

This is London 1/3/07

Carol fire fear

AN annual carol concert has been banned over fire safety fears. Members of Castleford's Choral Society were stunned when managers at the town's Carlton Lanes shopping centre told them their event had been stopped after fire officers raised fears that the 30 members would block emergency exits. West Yorkshire Fire Service officers are now working with shopping centre managers to find a solution to the problem. A spokeswoman said: 'We advised that there were some concerns with some of the stands that they wanted to use, and alongside the carol singers this may cause a risk to fire escape procedures,' she said. 'These concerns were raised purely in the interest of public safety, which is of course our overall priority.'

BBC News 10/12/04

Lollipop licked

CALLS for a lollipop lady on a busy road in Huddersfield have been rejected because it is too dangerous. Stunned parents argued that was why they wanted a crossing patrol there in the first place. But a council's highways chiefs denied the request on 'Health and Safety grounds' and said it was down to mums and dads to get kids to school safely. The lollipop lady would have helped pupils going to Reinwood Community Junior School in Marsh, Huddersfield, West Yorks. School head Graham Altoft said: 'It seems bizarre. What about the health and safety of the children crossing the road?'

The Sun 16/11/06

Danger, men sitting

BRITISH Airways has been accused of treating all men passengers as potential sex offenders after it was revealed it has
banned children from sitting next to male strangers – even if
their parents are on the same flight. The bizarre regulation
came to light when a nine-year-old girl was moved from her
seat next to a 76-year-old passenger and his wife on a flight
from Malaga to London. Instead, her mother was told by a
stewardess to take the seat next to retired journalist Michael
Kemp and his wife Frances, and the girl was moved to the
back of the plane. Mr Kemp said: 'To my amazement, the
stewardess said BA had a rule that no unaccompanied child
under 16 may be seated next to an adult male stranger – even
if there's a woman on the other side. Leading child protection
campaigner Michele Elliot, director of the children's charity
Kidscape, said she was astonished by the BA rule. 'It is utterly
absurd. It brands all men as potential sex offenders,' she said.
'What message does it send out to children – that men are not
to be trusted? Women also abuse children. This is just totally
lacking in common sense.'

Daily Mail 4/11/06

Tatty Ted alarm

A new warning has been issued to parents and teddy bear
collectors in Edinburgh over the safety of their stuffed toys.
Geraldine Elliott, of the shop and doll's hospital on the
Canongate, Edinburgh, warned that elderly bears stuffed with
foam that does not meet modern safety standards can be a
'serious fire hazard'. She said: 'I've no doubt the vast majority

of people who own teddies don't realise how serious the health risk is to themselves should the worst happen and a teddy catch fire. All bears, and especially those aged 30 to 35 years, that have foam inside them should come into the hospital for appropriate treatment.'

The Scotsman 3/1/07

Train outing off

A train company has apologised to a group of children after it refused to carry them on a school trip to Rhyl saying it feared they might present a Health and Safety risk. More than 50 five- and six-year-olds from the school in Dawley near Telford, Shropshire, were forced to go to the coast by coach after Wales and Border Trains said there were too many of them to accommodate. The train company has admitted the school did not receive the level of service it deserved and has now offered the children a free trip to the seaside. But the head teacher of St Leonard's Infants School said they have not yet decided to accept the offer. The 54 youngsters had been preparing for the geography and history trip to the seaside for months. 'Many of our children have never gone to the coast or on a train before,' said head teacher Lorraine Campbell. 'We've had videos showing the children beaches and train platforms. It was going to be a very exciting day for the children. They were very disappointed.'

BBC News 12/6/03

A council leader has overturned a decision to ban a bubble machine at his regular hairdresser's. Jacqui Langner was ordered to remove a £50 promotional gimmick outside her salon by council inspectors who claimed that bubbles blown at passers-by were a safety hazard. But Councillor Mark Hunter – himself a regular customer – has slammed the decision as nonsensical. Jacqui, whose husband Stephen suggested the bubble machine after using it on a pub dance floor, said: 'We had a lot of response from the general public when it was switched off and people have been coming in to set up petitions. Now that the bubbles are back on, people are banging on the widows to say well done. We were thinking of having a snow machine in the winter months, so we will have to see what the council say.'

Manchester Evening News 30/8/02

THROWING bonbons and boiled sweets into the audience has been a tradition of the festive pantomime for decades. But bureaucrats are set to stamp out the tradition because they claim boiled sweets could injure a member of the audience. Instead, organisers of one pantomime have been told they must go down into the crowd and hand out the sweets. The ruling was made by a committee for the Preston Drama Club in Lancashire, which fears an injury could spark a compensation claim. Committee members believe it would be far too costly to insure against a member of the audience losing an eye or sustaining another injury. But some members of the group have branded the move as 'ridiculous' and say Health and Safety restrictions are killing tradition in Britain. Don Stephenson, president of Preston Drama Club, said: 'There are so many rules and regulations now we were not really surprised because this is just another one. These are only sweets, they wouldn't hurt anybody.'

Evening Standard 12/12/06

Watch out!

A girl of six has been banned from wearing a Barbie watch to school after a teacher decided that fellow pupils might be scratched by the metal winder when she put her hand up to answer a question. The girl had been given the watch by her parents so she could learn to tell the time. Hampshire County Council said: 'The teacher may have been overzealous.'

Derbygripe.co.uk 2/07

Fear of fruit

ORANGE pips and plum stones have become the latest concern for Health and Safety enthusiasts, a report reveals. Some schools, which are giving out free fruit to their pupils under a health initiative funded by the Scottish Executive, believe that fruits with pips are dangerous and so are avoiding them. 'We tend not to use stone fruits because of the safety issues. Orange pips fall into that category,' a respondent to the study said. As well as worrying that children would choke to death, some teachers were concerned that they could slip over on dropped fruit, or be allergic to it. A spokesman for the Executive said the children were still receiving free fruit, whether it had pips in or not. 'It is up to individual schools what fruit is served,' he said. 'The important thing is that children eat it.' Fiona Hyslop, the SNP shadow education minister, said the move risked giving children a fear of fruit. 'This is like the nanny state gone mad,' she said. According to the report, 14 per cent of respondents had some fears over Health and Safety issues. Most worrying were the hygiene aspects of preparing, storing and handling the fruit.

Daily Telegraph 9/1/06

First-aid fiasco

A parent has spoken of his anger after his wife had to go to their daughter's school to put a plaster on when staff said they were not allowed to. Julie Scott, 38, was called by staff at Uphill Primary School near Weston-super-Mare, after her daughter Emily, nine, cut her finger. The school said strict guidelines meant they were not allowed to give plasters. The head says the school is to review their interpretation to make sure they take a 'common sense approach'. Mrs Scott travelled the short distance to the school, bandaged her daughter's finger and left a box of plasters by her desk in case of any 'further mishaps'. Staff at the school told Mrs Scott that local council guidelines meant they were unable to put the sticking plaster on Emily's cut finger. But Emily's father Kevan, 39, criticised the guidelines. He said: 'The whole saga is absolutely ridiculous. My daughter had a tiny cut and I just cannot see the reason why a plaster couldn't be put on her finger by the staff.'

BBC News 11/3/06

Fireman's lift

FIRE chiefs have been slammed for banning tots from sitting in their fire engines. Devon Fire Service fears staff could be falsely accused of inappropriate behaviour when lifting kids out of trucks during nursery visits. A spokesman said: 'It's sad, but we must protect crews.'

The People 4/2/07

Height of lunacy

STAFF at Britain's most secure mental hospital have been banned from hanging Xmas decorations unless they have height training. NHS workers at Broadmoor have been told not to stretch 'above normal reach from the floor' unless they are qualified. They must have attended a 'working at height' course or face disciplinary action. A worker who saw the warning on a noticeboard said: 'The lunatics really are running the asylum. Too many managers have too little to do with their time. It's making us a laughing stock.' Broadmoor is one of dozens of hospitals and clinics run by West London Mental Health NHS Trust. All 4000 workers face the same extraordinary ruling. The Trust said: 'The aim is to protect staff. We have a duty to make them aware of Health and Safety regulations.'

The Sun 21/12/06

Flying saucer ban

THE tradition of smashing plates at Greek restaurants is disappearing because of a 'compensation culture' which

91

hundreds of owners fear will lead to them being sued by customers hit by flying crockery. 'It's a nice Greek tradition, but what can you do?' said Chris Toumaz, who runs Trios in Palmers Green, north London. 'All these claims now, everyone's just looking for an excuse to sue you. We have stopped doing it.' Some restaurateurs have replaced plates with less dramatic alternatives. 'We're throwing flowers now,' said Nikos Constantinou, the manager of the Apollo Restaurant Taverna, in Islington, north London. 'It's not as messy and if you hit someone, it doesn't really matter.' Safety inspectors said that the restaurateurs were right to be cautious. Jenny Morris, the food policy officer at the Chartered Institute of Environmental Health, said: 'It's one of those things that seem great fun, but there are hidden dangers to it. Plate shards can do quite a bit of damage, especially to the eye. You also have the potential for shards of crockery to go into food.'

Daily Telegraph 23/11/03

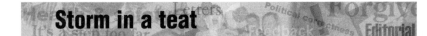

Storm in a teat

A mother has hit out at a fast-food restaurant after it refused to let her warm up a bottle of milk for her baby, who suffers from a rare brain condition. Susan Farrell was shocked when staff at KFC in Craigleith Retail Park told her they could not provide her with hot water to warm a bottle for her 18-week-old daughter Charlotte. It also refused to heat up the milk in their kitchen for what staff said were 'Health and Safety' reasons. Miss Farrell, 33, a financial advisor from Livingston, had stopped at the restaurant for coffee while out shopping. She said: 'All I asked for was a cup of hot water so I could heat it up at the table. We were having hot coffee, so I can't see how it was a safety risk. The milk was in a sealed bottle, so there was no risk of contamination. We had to take it across the road to Sainsbury's, who warmed it up straight away. It's just ludicrous.'

The Scotsman 3/1/07

Mr Punch KO'd

GENERATIONS of youngsters have been thrilled by the slapstick excesses of the traditional Punch and Judy show, but killjoy Newcastle City Council bosses delivered a KO blow after claims it could encourage domestic violence. The performance by popular children's entertainer Bo the Clown was part of a Council-sponsored arts event to encourage children to express themselves. But organisers stepped in following a complaint that the show might contain scenes of domestic violence, and pulled the curtain down on Mr Punch. Bo, real name Derek Carpenter, hit back and demanded to know what was wrong with his act. 'I will be happy if I can get to speak to the person who made the complaint and hopefully allay their fears,' he said. 'There doesn't appear to be any evidence that Punch and Judy causes violence. On the contrary, there is evidence that it can help children express themselves.' Greg Stone, chairman of the city's Liberal Democrats, said: 'This is ludicrous. It's evidence of the council's killjoy attitude.' North East Tory MEP Martin

Callanan added: 'Clearly, this is the work of some politically correct left-wing zealot, and I'm amazed senior civic centre staff have taken this seriously.'

Evening Chronicle, Newcastle 21/8/02

Cheese off

GLOUCESTERSHIRE'S annual cheese-rolling contest has been cancelled because the safety team is away in Algeria helping victims of an earthquake. The traditional event involves scores of people chasing a seven-pound Double Gloucester 200 yards down a steep slope near the town. Thousands gather to watch the spectacle, which has taken place most years for the past two centuries. Tony Tizard, chairman of the organisers, said: 'We are very disappointed to have to cancel at the last minute. St John Ambulance have also had to withdraw their services because without the extra cover they can't rescue anyone from the slope.' Although they can provide cover at the bottom of the hill, their insurance does not cover them to rescue off the hillside, he added. There have been previous attempts to ban the cheese-rolling race because of the number of injuries.

BBC News 25/5/03

Paedo phone ban

THE latest picture mobile phones have been banned from Bolton Council Sports Centre changing rooms – to stop paedophiles taking photos of children undressing. Town Hall bosses fear perverts are using the new-generation phones to snap children in swimming pools and changing areas. Images can then be sent to other phones or e-mailed to a computer or laptop and posted on the Internet minutes after they are taken. Bolton Council is the first in Greater Manchester to ban picture mobiles in all its sport centres and pools. Picture phone users will be asked to hand in their mobiles at reception, and will even be asked to leave if they persist in using the handsets.

Manchester Evening News 20/5/03

Diana paddle peril

THE Diana, Princess of Wales Memorial Fountain, which suffered a catalogue of teething problems, is to reopen to the public but access will be managed and visitors will no longer be allowed to walk in the water. The fountain was shut down after three consecutive slippage incidents. Under the new guidelines, drawn up with the help of the Royal Society for the Prevention of Accidents, people will be asked not to walk or run in the water. However, they will be allowed to paddle their feet and dip their hands while sitting on the sides of the £3.6 million feature in Hyde Park, central London. Originally, visitors were invited to paddle in the water which pours into the large granite ring and flows in two directions to 'reflect the turbulence, excitement and energy in Diana's life'. Temporary fences will also be erected around the memorial over a one-hectare area fitted with gates to allow staff to manage the number of people visiting the fountain at any given time. Signs will explain the memorial guidelines to the public.

Evening Standard 11/8/04

Backstroke ban

SWIMMERS at a council-run pool have been barred from doing backstroke at busy times because it is considered too dangerous. Daisyfield Swimming Pool in Blackburn is understood to be one of the first in the country to introduce such a move. It is hoped the ruling will prevent any legal action against the council if a swimmer collides with someone. It follows the publication of new guidelines – suggested by the Institute of Sport and Recreation Management. Steve Rigby, Executive Director of Culture, Leisure and Sport at Blackburn with Darwen Borough Council, said: 'Lane swimming at Daisyfield Pool is proving very popular. This has resulted in us requesting that people do not swim back-stroke during these busy sessions, in order to avoid any dangerous collisions.' The previous year, a water polo team was banned from practising at the venue because of the fear that stray balls were a danger to the players.

BBC News 22/3/04

In the dark

FIVE thousand people joined a town's Christmas lights countdown but there were no lights to switch on. They were taken down for safety reasons a week previously after one string of bulbs fell into the street, but the organisers had the bright idea of going ahead with the switch-on anyway. The event in Colchester, Essex, had been billed as the 'biggest-ever parade and town light switch-on'. It included children marching through the streets with Father Christmas, the chance to meet Colchester United players, and youngsters decorating a tree. But as the countdown reached zero, the only lights that flickered into action were in shop windows and on a Christmas tree. Chris Rawlinson, of the Colchester Town Partnership, said: 'Two of the cross-street features fell, but nobody was injured. We took them all down for safety reasons.'

Daily Mirror 6/11/06

Bus stop for choc

A diabetic was left shivering in the cold for half an hour after a bus driver refused to let her on board with a cup of hot chocolate. Heather Wallace, of New Cheveley Road, Newmarket, said she was appalled by the Stagecoach driver's insensitive ban as she tried to catch a bus from Cambridge on her way home from Addenbrooke's Hospital. She said: 'I have to go to Addenbrooke's a lot, and as a diabetic I often need a sweet drink to keep my blood sugar stable, so I normally carry a flask.' But Alan Woods, operation manager for Stagecoach, defended the ban, saying: 'The company would be held liable for damages if movement on the bus caused a passenger to spill hot liquid on themselves or another person.'

Cambridge Evening News 30/11/04

PALLBEARERS are being asked to sign waiver forms in case they hurt their backs carrying the coffin into church. Funeral directors are so worried about them slipping a disc and then suing for compensation that they are insisting relatives or friends who want to shoulder the coffin confirm in writing before the ceremony starts that they are aware of the risk. Dominic Maguire, of the National Association of Funeral Directors, said: 'Funeral directors should use their discretion, but I expect this to become a routine procedure in the near future.'

Mail on Sunday 3/12/06

CHILDREN have been banned from making daisy chains and playing with yo-yos because school bosses say the games are too dangerous. Handstands, tag and climbing frames have also been halted in case they hurt themselves, warned the Children's Society, which described the edicts as 'ludicrous'. A London primary school outlawed daisy chains in case kids picked up germs. Some parks and playgrounds even prevented kids from playing in bushes in case they got 'too dirty'. Researchers from the Society quizzed more than 500 children, who said that playgrounds had become too boring. Half had been stopped from playing with water, a third were told not to climb trees in parks and playgrounds, and a quarter were banned from riding skateboards or climbing frames. Tim Gill, director of the Children's Play Council said: 'Trying to guarantee absolute safety is not doing the best for kids. The real world is not risk-free.'

The Sun 29/7/02

Glowstick procession

TORCHES have been banned from a festive torchlight procession because of Health and Safety fears. Marchers couldn't even carry candles in case people with long hair caught fire. Instead, councillors in the Cornish harbour town of Looe spent £350 on 500 plastic glowsticks for the event. Mayor Ron Overd said: 'These days, people are suing at the drop of a hat. What we are talking about is naked flames, hot wax, long hair, cars with wax sprayed on them. We decided it would be prudent to use some other form of lighting.'

Derbygripe.co.uk 2/07

Too many toddlers

A lifeguard instructor and her husband have been banned from taking their three children into the toddlers' pool at Sedgemoor Splash in Bridgwater, Somerset. Keren and David Townsend were told their children needed individual supervision.

Daily Mail 24/4/06

Alarm bells

A mediaeval village church could be forced to silence its bells which have chimed for 200 years following a single complaint. A resident is claiming the bells at St Cuthbert's Church in Halsall, Lancashire, are keeping children awake at night. The complaint was made to the council after the clock was restored after a year out of action. The Rev. Paul Robinson said: 'We've been told it's a noise nuisance so we may have to stop the chimes completely or switch them off during certain times. If the Christian faith is about anything, it is how we live as a community, not this society, which is all "me, me, me".' A spokeswoman for West Lancashire District Council said: 'The council has no choice but to take heed of the national legislation, which demands that any complaints are fully investigated and that formal action is taken where necessary.'

BBC News 12/1/07

Tree fellers wanted

PEOPLE in Usk thought vandals had chopped down their £125 Christmas tree – sawing it into four pieces – just a week before Father Christmas was to visit the picturesque town.

Police were told about it and issued a public appeal for witnesses who had seen what happened to the 20 ft tree. But it was red faces all around when Monmouthshire County Council told police one of their workers had sawn up the tree after it had been blown down in high winds. Mayor of Usk, Kay Peacock, said the council will now fork out another £125 for a replacement tree in time for the visit by Father Christmas. 'It's a shame,' she said. 'But hopefully a new tree will be delivered and we can get it up quickly.'

South Wales Argus 4/12/06

Pansies in strain concern

GARDENERS working for Cheltenham Council, Gloucestershire, have been banned from planting pansies under town centre trees because workers digging with trowels risked spraining their wrists in the root-filled soil.

The Times 18/4/06

Flag jam

FIREFIGHTERS have been stopped from repairing a flagpole for veterans planning a Remembrance Sunday parade. The old soldiers were told that the firemen could not climb a ladder up the 35 ft pole in a non-emergency because of Health and Safety regulations.

Members of the Royal British Legion in Carshalton, Surrey, discovered that they would be unable to raise a flag because a rope was snagged on a pulley. As most were in their 70s, 80s and 90s and too old to climb up to fix the problem themselves, they turned to their local fire station. David Plattern, 56, secretary of Carshalton Royal British Legion Club, said: 'The lads at the fire station were more than happy to help. But their station officer said it was against Health and Safety regulations, as they can only use high ladders in an emergency. I thought he was joking at first but then I realised he was serious.

It is Health and Safety madness, just another sign of the barmy society we're living in today.' Stan Graves, an 84-year-old Burma veteran, threatened to climb the flagpole and get deliberately stuck so that the fire brigade would have to rescue him. He said: 'We would have dialled 999 and asked the fire brigade to save me. We could have got them to fix the flagpole while they were up there.'

Daily Telegraph 4/11/06

Boxed out

THEY add colour to a dreary world and provide a tiny garden for their owners. But window boxes have now been identified by an insurance company as potentially dangerous, and as a result people living in flats in east London have been told to remove them from their ledges. A letter from James Kirkwood, general manager of the Bow Quarter, said the pots had been categorised as an 'avoidable event' by insurer Norwich Union and must be taken down unless they were tightly secured. Failure to comply with the order would result in the forcible removal of pots and window boxes during 'the next window cleaning cycle', they were told. Resident Joanne Moore said she had been forced to remove her geraniums as a result of the order. 'Living in a flat, you don't have a garden,' she said. 'The flowers that we had in the pots really brightened the place up.'

This is London 26/10/04

Fish 'n' chip chop

THE boss of a Wakefield chip shop is being probed by town hall officials because his shop smells of 'fish and chips'. Environmental health staff wrote to Steve Morton to say they were investigating an 'odour from the extract ventilation system'. He was told: 'We are investigating a smell of fish and chips.' The council is monitoring the odours and told Steve he could be banned from having fish and chip smells in his chippy, which has been operating without a problem for 40 years. A council spokesman said: 'We have a duty to investigate complaints.'

The Sun 7/11/06

Fête fear

A village fête has been told it must commission a risk assessment before its local choir is allowed to sing in the parish church. Terrington in North Yorkshire is planning a grand celebration next summer to mark ten years of work by its local arts group, with All Saints Church a key venue. But the festival's steering committee has been told that before it can go ahead it must carry out detailed assessments of every potential risk in every location across the village where the scores of events will be held. Ian Hughes, the village postmaster and one of the organisers, said: 'I guess that's how life is these days. It's because of the culture we live in where the slightest thing can get you sued.'

Derbygripe.co.uk 2/07

Too cool for school

INFANT school pupils have been banned from taking off their sweatshirts in the heatwave sunshine unless their parents sign a consent form first. They even have to wear their long-sleeved jumpers during PE unless they have written permission to peel off. The move is to prevent pupils from suffering sunburn and sunstroke, yet has been blasted as 'the nanny-state gone mad'.

Daily Mirror 7/6/06

Threat to yew

A COUNCIL has removed up to 100 yew trees planted near a playground following complaints from parents that children could be poisoned if they ate the leaves or berries.

The trees were planted last year at a cost of about £1000 at the area on the Blaise Castle estate in Bristol, which is managed by the city council. But council workers have now ripped up the 4 ft high trees. The council said that following a 'risk assessment' it was decided that the 'safest option' was to remove them. But one mother said the council was being over-cautious. Helen Santry, 52, a nurse, said: 'To cut down these beautiful young trees seems absolutely ludicrous. There are hundreds of adult yew trees around the estate, not to mention deadly nightshade in the woods and poisonous fungi.' Trevor Beer, a naturalist, said it would take 'handfuls' of the plant to present a danger. 'That is no excuse to uproot them. If that happened to all Britain's poisonous plants, there would be no countryside left.'

Daily Telegraph 30/3/06

THE traditional children's party game of musical chairs has been accused of breeding violence. A booklet launched by the Education Minister Margaret Hodge says nursery schools should consider playing a less aggressively competitive game – such as musical statues. The booklet *Towards a Non-Violent Society*, produced by the Forum on Children and Violence, argues that musical chairs only rewards the 'strongest and fastest'. The Department for Education says that the booklet 'advises that teachers might think of less confrontational alternatives'. But the Conservative education spokeswoman Theresa May slammed the safety advice. 'Children have played and enjoyed musical chairs for years,' she said. 'This is yet more interference by a government, not content with just telling teachers what to do, they are now telling children what games they can and cannot play.'

BBC News 23/5/2000

Plain daff

FLOWER-loving Jenny Bailey was barred from planting daffodils outside a tax office on Health and Safety grounds. Gardening fan Jenny, in her 60s, wanted to brighten up the patch of land with some bulbs she had spare. She was stunned when officials vetoed the idea because she might injure herself and sue them. Jenny, who has planted flowers in her neighbourhood for 30 years, said: 'It's crazy. What is the world coming to?' Green-fingered Jenny is regularly employed by her local council in Stroud, Gloucestershire, to spruce up the town. 'I don't know how they think I am going to injure myself,' she said. 'With 30 years experience, it's insulting.'

The Sun 27/12/04

Veteran's liability

WAR veterans across the country have reacted with outrage as Remembrance parades are targeted by Health and Safety killjoys. They have been told the marches cannot go ahead unless they take out public liability insurance, carry out a risk assessment, and organise stewards dressed in fluorescent jackets to police the event. Many associations may be forced to cancel ceremonies because of the time and cost of complying with the barmy regulations. North Yorkshire Police said this was the first year they had implemented the stricter rules. 'We are concerned with the safety of everyone involved in the parade, including those taking part, spectators, and our own officers,' a spokesman said. 'All event organisers must comply with Health and Safety legislation for both their protection and that of the general public. Without it, the organisers would be held personally liable for any injuries or damage caused as a result of the parade.' But veterans say the politically correct edicts are an insult to their comrades who died fighting fascism. Association chairman Peter Lee-Hale said: 'The whole thing is ridiculous. We're only marching less than a mile. We went to war to fight fascism, but it's our police who are acting like Hitler.'

Sunday Express 8/9/06

Black day for naan

BLOWTORCHES used to give naan bread its traditional blackened coating are to be banned from Scotland's Asian restaurants on health grounds. In a new safety crackdown, environmental health officers are disconnecting the traditional equipment after fears that staff and customers are being put at risk from carbon monoxide poisoning and the threat of gas explosions. But many restaurant owners say the blowtorches pose no greater risk than conventional methods. And they claim banning them is an over-reaction that would spoil the quality of naan they served up. Sarfaraz Rathore, owner of the King's Balti in Buccleuch Street, said he had never heard of an accident with the torches after 20 years in the business, adding he was one of the first restaurants visited by environmental health officers, who disconnected his blowtorch and confiscated it. A spokeswoman for the city council's environmental health department said: 'These blowtorches are not very safe and restaurants are not allowed to use them unless they have a proper certificate.'

The Scotsman 13/10/03

No TV for OAPs

ELDERLY hospital patients missed out on TV over Christmas
when Health and Safety bosses banned all sets from wards on
the grounds that they posed a hazard. The order was imposed
at Penrhos Stanley Community Hospital in Holyhead, Anglesey,
after Health and Safety inspectors visited the ward where its
small number of mainly elderly inpatients are staying. Patients
have been allowed to have their own portable televisions and
video or DVD players by their beds since the complex was
built ten years ago, but bosses maintain the trailing leads 'could
lead to trips and falls' and say patients will have to go to the
lounge if they want to watch their favourite programmes.

Mail on Sunday 10/12/06

Stars out

THE Burma Star Association has been banned from selling
Remembrance Day poppies in Derby's Eagle Centre after their
stall was branded a fire risk. The local branch has set up a
stall in the centre for several years, but the centre management
said the group were unable to do the same thing this year for
Health and Safety reasons. Julie Ralphs, from the centre, said:
'There is a lot of work going on in the centre at the moment
and we have really had to tighten up on our health and safety.
It would have been acceptable before, but we are having to
keep all areas quite clear at the moment. It is unfortunate
that we have been unable to accommodate them at this time.'
A neighbouring indoor market and shop have stepped in to
allow the association to put up two stalls.

BBC News 8/11/06

Junk the cheese

CHEESE is to be treated as junk food under new advertising rules for children's television. The rules are part of a government drive to reduce children's exposure to foods high in fat, salt and sugar. Much to the disgust of its makers, cheese is to be regarded in the same light as crisps, sugary cereals and cheeseburgers. The Food Standards Agency model assesses the fat, sugar and salt content in a 100 g or 100 ml serving of food or drink. But the British Cheese Board points out that a typical portion of cheese was 30–40 g, not the 100 g used in the Agency's model. The National Farmers' Union described the decision as 'nannying gone mad'. And Mary Quicke, who runs Quicke's Cheese in Devon, producing handmade cheddar, said the rules had left her 'speechless'. She told BBC Radio 4's Today programme: 'Frankly, it's bonkers.' She said the FSA's decision to assess cheese using a 100 g portion was ridiculous. 'Imagine eating 100 grams of cheese – that's four ounces. You would have to be a pretty dedicated eater of cheese.'

Daily Mail 3/1/07

Careful carers

A woman aged 99 has been told that carers cannot help her climb the stairs in case she injures them in a fall. Edna East, a 4 ft 9 ins great-grandmother who weighs seven stone, has had to spends hundreds of pounds on a stairlift after being told she was a threat to carers' safety. Her daughter, Suzanne Singer, said: 'How ludicrous can you get?' The carers' job was surely to ensure Mrs East's safety, she said. 'To say they can't help her because of a possible injury risk is barmy. How risky is it to help an elderly woman up the stairs? She's never fallen before. It's stupid, mindless bureaucracy.' After a care provision risk assessment, Mrs Singer received a letter from Enara Community Care, which is contracted by Oxfordshire County Council and visits clients in the morning and evening. Sandra Stapley, the council's operations manager for adult social care, said: 'This is not a case of health and safety gone mad. This is a case of a care provider deciding, after carrying out at least two risk assessments, that supporting a frail, unsteady elderly lady up and down the stairs was unsafe for both herself and their staff.'

The Times 14/10/06

Danger eggs

CHILDREN have been banned from collecting chickens' eggs at the National Trust's showpiece farm at Wimpole Hall in Cambridgeshire because it is now deemed by Health and Safety advisers to be too hazardous.

Daily Telegraph 17/5/05

Band banned

FOR more than a century Stanhope Town Band has marched through the town's main street each year to herald the start of Stanhope Show. But police have cancelled the latest parade on safety grounds, saying they hadn't been informed it would happen. Now furious musicians and politicians have attacked Durham Police's killjoy approach. Band leader and conductor Steve Robson said: 'It was very disappointing. I believe strongly in tradition. For as long as anyone can remember a band has marched through the town and then walked across the stepping stones before marching into the showfield.' But Sgt Jon Curtis of Crook Police insisted the long arm of the law were not killjoys, saying: 'For health and safety and litigation purposes we had to turn the request down on this occasion. There was simply insufficient time to plan the march and close the road.'

The Journal, Newcastle, 18/9/02

Killer cream cakes

THE school cake stall, a quaint feature of summer fêtes for generations, has become the latest tradition to fall to the 'compensation culture'. Lisa Tudor, head of Crudwell Primary School in Wiltshire, has banned home-cooked cakes from her fête in case they cause food poisoning. In a letter to parents, Ms Tudor said that the decision was made after taking advice from the local county council and had been backed by school governors. But John Thompson, a Conservative councillor for the school's area, ridiculed the ban. 'It's preposterous. The world is full of people at the moment blowing each other up and we're worried about killer cream cakes,' he said.

The Times 5/6/04

Egg risk

TO the patriots of Bromham, a hearty English breakfast seemed the perfect way to celebrate St George's Day. Some 300 villagers were planning to tuck in to the fry-up in their community centre. But the charity event was cancelled at the last minute – because of a Health and Safety warning against frying eggs. The local council's guidelines state that volunteers should not prepare 'protein-based foods' without proper training and the centre did not have the correct facilities to 'chill, prepare and store' the food. Faced with not being able to serve eggs, cheese or milk, organisers abandoned the event. They had been hoping to raise £500 for St Nicholas Primary School in the village near Chippenham, Wiltshire. Peter Wallis, 39, chairman of the school's parents and teachers association, said: 'I was astonished to discover that we had to adhere to Health and Safety regulations to cook people breakfast. This is just plain daft. These breakfasts have been going on for many years and we've never poisoned anyone.'

Daily Mail 24/4/06

Ramble risk

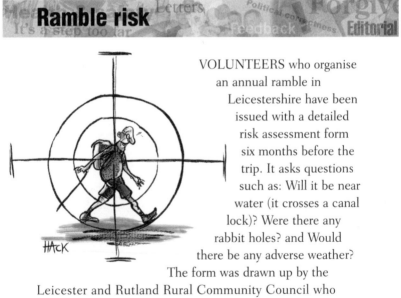

VOLUNTEERS who organise an annual ramble in Leicestershire have been issued with a detailed risk assessment form six months before the trip. It asks questions such as: Will it be near water (it crosses a canal lock)? Were there any rabbit holes? and Would there be any adverse weather? The form was drawn up by the Leicester and Rutland Rural Community Council who commissioned the walk. Officials say it is so walkers can be adequately insured. Colin Hames, from the Wigston Civic Society, which organises the yearly walk, said: 'We thought it strange because we didn't think it possible to fill in a form like this six months before we actually do the walk. It asked were there any ploughed fields, cows in a field, or anything like that, and things can change overnight never mind six months.' The route, called the Millennium Walk, is staged once a year by the volunteers on behalf of the Rural Community Council.

BBC Radio Leicester 7/2/05

Out of the swim

FOR more than 100 years swimmers have headed to Hampstead Heath for an early-morning dip in its icy ponds. Now the Corporation of London, which runs the heath, is set to ban unsupervised swimming. The corporation, which spends £600 000 a year employing 45 lifeguards to oversee the three bathing ponds and nearby Parliament Hill lido, says its members could personally face prosecution by the Health and Safety Executive if it permits unsupervised swimming and an incident occurs. Robert Sutherland Smith, chairman of the United Swimmers Association, said: 'We are not giving up on this. We do it not only for ourselves but also in the name of future generations.' He said there was no evidence of swimmers having come to difficulty in the ponds, which are free to use. His organisation offered to run a system of self-regulation before the lifeguards start work, but this is set to be rejected by the Corporation on legal advice.

Evening Standard 19/7/04

Court OKs wheelchair ban

A mum who sued her local council after her disabled son wasn't allowed into his brother's school in his wheelchair has failed in her High Court bid for massive damages.

Rebecca Lawrence claimed she was left distressed and humiliated by the ban enforced by Cambridgeshire County Council-controlled Monkfield Primary School in Cambourne. But Judge Hawkesworth QC said there had been no discrimination on the part of the school, and its actions had not made it 'unreasonable' for Mrs Lawrence to bring her twin son Matthew – who suffers from cerebral palsy – on to the premises. The judge added that the High Court was 'really not the place to determine issues like this' and said even if Matthew had been discriminated against he was so young that it could have had no real effect on him.

Cambridge Evening News 2/12/05

Dole tree danger

CIVIL servants have been ordered to take down Christmas trees because bosses fear irate job hunters might attack staff with an artificial 4 ft-high Norwegian spruce. Instructions to dismantle decorations were issued across Jobcentres in southeast London after warnings that they could be used as offensive weapons. The wire-and-nylon tree in the Greenwich Employment Exchange was put back in its box when it was officially deemed a Health and Safety threat. Bexleyheath has lost its fake spruce, and employees in the Deptford branch never even dusted down their fake shrub, after managers intervened to nip the tree in the bud. One manager told astonished workers: 'I don't want you coming to us when someone hits you with a tree.' An e-mail sent to Jobcentre staff by Lynda Russell, the southeast London district manager, all but cancels Christmas for the public sector. 'There will be no decorations in customer-facing offices and there will be no parties within any offices with alcohol,' she proclaimed.

The Guardian 13/12/03

Flame warning

CAPTAIN Tony Spacey, who sells honey and hive products at Derby's continental market, has been told by a trading standards officer he cannot sell candles unless he tells customers there is a risk they could start fires. Captain Spacey said a trading standards officer said his candles did not meet regulations. 'I was absolutely dumbfounded when I was told that I couldn't sell candles because they don't carry warnings. I thought that the whole point of lighting a candle was to have a fire on the top.' He was also told his jars of honey had to be labelled, otherwise he could not tell customers what was in them. He said: 'I was told that, unless we had it on the jar, we couldn't tell people what it was.'

Derbygripe.co.uk 2/07

Lottery hazard

A charity group has hit out at a ban on its fund-raising at a hospital – because its standing lottery display and mobile ticket trolley have been ruled potential fire hazards. The League of

Friends of Warrington Hospital has raised about £1m over 15 years. Friends' chairman Alan Woodward described the ban as 'a bombshell'. He said: 'The ban is nothing to do with the hospital. It is the fire brigade who have come in and told us our activities constitute a hazard.' He added a number of other charities had been affected by the ban, including Macmillan Nurses and the British Heart Foundation. A spokesman for Cheshire Fire Brigade said: 'One of our fire safety officers visited the hospital and inquired if the lottery stand, which has bright lights shining down on it, had been the subject of a risk assessment. We were told it had not.'

Manchester Evening News 25/5/04

Building block

A barmy building society has stopped using Lego to keep customers' children amused – because it says the toy is a health hazard. Bosses at the Saffron Walden, Herts and Essex Building Society told all 13 branches to remove the building bricks. One shocked mum who uses a branch at Ware, Hertfordshire, said: 'My son always plays with the Lego and went straight for where the toys usually are – but they had been cleared away. A cashier said they got rid of them all because of health and safety regulations. I was incensed. The world has gone crackers. I really couldn't believe what I was hearing.' A building society source said: 'They're worried about somebody tripping over a piece of Lego. It's just risk assessment gone mad.'

The Sun 28/4/06

PARENTS should be banned from videoing their children on school sports days in an attempt to keep the images out of the hands of paedophiles. The National Confederation of Parent Teacher Associations is now calling for a ban on all cameras and video equipment from school sports events.

Newcastle Sunday Sun 3/6/05

HACK

HUNDREDS of people celebrated Guy Fawkes night crowded around a virtual bonfire projected onto a giant screen after Health and Safety killjoys forced them to scrap the real thing. Officials at Ilfracombe Rugby Club haven't held a bonfire night for four years, since being put off by the mountain of paperwork and regulations set by council chiefs.

But this year they opted to show a film of the blaze instead to get round the strict rules surrounding the lighting of fires at public events. Club president Paul Crabb said: 'We always used to have a bonfire, but in the end it got too much. The number of bits of paper you have to wade through to hold a bonfire is just insane. I thought the idea was to light a fire and have a laugh – but the council are all "risk assessment" and "liability". All the fun went out of it.'

Evening Standard 3/11/06

Bad eggs

HALLOWE'EN egg throwers face prosecution, police have warned. Suffolk police have asked shopkeepers to ban the sale of eggs to youngsters between Sunday and Tuesday in a bid to prevent complaints about 'trick or treat' pests. There will be extra police patrols and the Suffolk force's helicopter will be used to check on revellers. As in previous years, the police are issuing posters for householders to display asking 'trick or treaters' to stay away.

Cambridge Evening News 27/10/06

High and dry

THE Environment Agency has stopped operating mill flood gates on the river made famous by the artist John Constable because it says the structures do not comply with modern Health and Safety standards. The ban applies to 18 cast-iron mill sluices on the Stour, Colne and Blackwater in Essex and Suffolk and some of their tributaries. Conservationists say that not operating the sluices has emptied 18 miles of the Stour, with implications for wildlife habitat, fishing, and the control of watermeadows where the water levels have been managed for at least 1000 years. Adrian Walters, of the Sudbury Common Lands Charity, which manages 210 acres of river bank on either side of the Stour in Sudbury, said the decision initially to leave one of the flood gates open had a drastic impact on wildlife. 'The whole ecosystem was compromised when the water dropped away,' he said. 'There were snails left high and dry and sticklebacks in small pools, some dead and others dying.'

Daily Telegraph 6/11/06

Toast burns

MUMS from the Pat-a-Cake Playgroup in Rawmarsh, South Yorkshire, are furious after being banned from serving tea and toast on Health and Safety grounds. The group, which caters for up to ten children, have been barred by their local council from having snacks during their weekly sessions. If they fail to follow the edict they could end up losing their free playtime at the local library. Julie Brown, 44, a mother-of-two who runs the group, said: 'We have been told the ban on tea and toast is to do with the council's Health and Safety policy. Tea and toast are very popular and other toddler groups do this. The children love a slice of toast.'

Daily Mail 9/2/07

Butt out bacon

A sandwich shop has been banned from selling bacon butties after a vegetarian complained about the 'vile' smell. Sizzlers Sandwich Bar in Stamford Square, Ashton under Lyne, was issued with an enforcement notice following complaints from neighbour Anthony Goodwin. Owners Steven and Linda Male have been warned by health officers they will be committing a criminal offence if they carry on making the traditional break-fast favourite, which they sell to customers for £1. The couple have described the order banning them from selling hot food as 'completely ridiculous' and say it will have a major impact on their livelihood.

Manchester Evening News 31/3/05

Too tall to party

Editorial

A tearful girl was banned from a children's birthday party by Jobsworth pub staff for being a quarter-inch too tall. Katie Best, 10, was looking forward to playing on slides and swings with pals at her six-year-old cousin's party. But she was left sobbing when a staff member said she was just over their 4 ft 9 ins restriction and had to leave. Distraught Katie had to sit on her own. She didn't even get a proper lunch after bungling staff refused to cook her a vegetarian meal and gave her a bowl of chips instead. Katie's fuming mum Sarah, 37, of Chadderton, near Oldham, said: 'My sister, who organised the party, was even told by Jobsworth staff she could not take pictures of her son blowing his candles out. The whole thing was a shambles.'

The Sun 6/5/06

Hot pants

Editorial

BINMEN in Fife struggling to cope with soaring temperatures have been threatened with dismissal if they wear shorts to work. Fife Council told refuse staff that if they did not wear long trousers they could be dismissed for failing to comply with Health and Safety rules. The council said that, as a responsible employer, it had to guard against staff suffering sunburn, scratches, cuts and insect bites while at work. A spokesman for the Dunfermline Refuse Workers' Union said: 'We have worn shorts in the summer for 15 years without a problem, but now the council will not budge because of new Health and Safety laws.'

The Times 15/6/05

Pulling a cracker

POLITICALLY correct killjoys have pulled festive fun off
the menu this Christmas by banning crackers. Bureaucrats
have branded the seasonal novelties 'dangerous objects',
because they contain gunpowder and are classed as explosives.
High-street giant Marks & Spencer has banned under-16s
from buying crackers at their stores because of safety fears.
Mum-of-three Natasha Burt, of Stillington, Teesside, who
was asked to verify her age by a shop assistant at a branch
of M&S at Monks Cross, York, declared the government
legislation 'political correctness gone mad'.

Newcastle Sunday Sun 18/12/05

Get the point

A primary school has banned plastic pencil sharpeners after
kids smashed them to get the blades out. Education bosses
claimed the youngsters at Normanton Junior School, Derby,
were just 'messing about'. Schools boss Andrew Flack said
there was 'no indication' that the children were using the
sharp objects as weapons. He said: 'Some of the children had
ground their heels into the sharpeners and taken the blades.
It was messing about.' The plastic sharpeners were removed
on Health and Safety grounds, he added. Head teacher
Dorcas Jennings said the incident was just 'silly behaviour' and
not sinister. She said each class now had one desk sharpener,
which pupils must queue to use.

Derby Evening Telegraph 22/2/06

Up in smoke

REVELLERS are facing bonfire night without a bonfire after killjoy council chiefs said it would cause air pollution. Watford Borough Council said it was dropping the traditional fire as part of the commemoration of the Guy Fawkes gunpowder plot as it went against its policy of a smoke-free town. Chiefs also admitted Health and Safety fears played a part in their decision, because of worries of overcrowding and the difficulties of putting out the blaze. Fireworks night in Cassiobury Park in the Hertfordshire town will now go ahead for the first time in 38 years without the usual bonfire.

Evening Standard 1/10/06

Raw deal

SCOTS butchers have vowed to defy a meddling Eurocrat who is trying to ruin their traditional mince and tatties. Brussels health commissioner Markos Kyprianou has banned butchers from making mince with properly aged beef. For generations, Scots butchers have made sure their mince has plenty of flavour by using beef that has been hung for up to three weeks. But the Cypriot wants to make sure French foodies don't poison themselves when they eat raw steak tartare. Scotland's meat producers say his edict threatens to make traditional mince tough and tasteless. Andy McGowan, of trade body Quality Meat Scotland, said: 'The new rule is clumsy and it will have a major impact on one of Scotland's favourite meals.' Leading butcher Duncan McKenzie, president of the Scottish Federation of Meat Traders Association, said Kyprianou's order was 'European bureaucracy gone crazy and butchers are being made to suffer.'

The Daily Record 13/7/06

122

Police hazard lights

SCROOGE police chiefs in the northeast have banned Christmas lights from police stations, claiming they are too dangerous. Durham Constabulary bosses sent out a force-wide memo telling officers not to put up the decorations because they were a risk to staff and the public. Steve Smith, chairman of the Durham Police Federation, said: 'I think it's a bit "Bah, humbug!" myself. I think it's over the top.' But a Durham Police spokesman said the decision was made to protect officers and the public from possible faulty lights.

A memo was circulated to all officers and station staff in the Durham area by the force's director of finance, Patrick Melia. It told force members that after a meeting of senior staff there was to be a blanket ban on electrical decorations, due to the fire risk.

Bosses say the ban is not down to the force refusing to spend money safety-testing the lights, but because of not knowing where lights would be put up and which ones were safe.

Newcastle Evening Chronicle 20/12/06

Put those lights out

TWO seaside towns have had to scrap Christmas lights because of new safety rules. Council chiefs told traders only qualified electricians were allowed to put up the festive decorations. That would have cost £2000 in Harwich, Essex. Neighbouring Dovercourt faced a £10 000 bill. Traders can't afford to pay. Pub boss Jamie Shrive, who put up Harwich's lights for ten years, said: 'I'm disappointed.' Essex County Council said: 'These are national guidelines under the Code of Practice for Installation, Operation and Removal of Seasonal Decorations.'

The Sun 6/10/06

Don't say it with flowers

MOURNERS at a Cambridge cemetery have been banned from leaving flowers in memento vases by Health and Safety officers after a child cut himself. Mrs Penny Binge, who has been leaving flowers at the cemetery for the past 21 years, said: 'I was horrified to read that after a child was injured it had been decided that all vases and mementos would be removed from the crematorium. I think this is outrageous. I urge the city council to stop and think about what you are doing to the millions of bereaved people, whose only place to go for their loved ones and take some flowers or a gift is the crematorium. Better still, put up a notice banning unruly children!'

Cambridge Evening News 2/2/07

Balls of disobedience

A row has broken out after children were suspended from school – for throwing snowballs. Shocked parents could not believe it when the youngsters were sent home from Bretton Woods Community School in Peterborough. Head teacher John Gribble defended the ban, saying the rules had been introduced for Health and Safety reasons. But parents said the 'laughable' exclusion of six or seven boys aged between 15 and 16 for playing in the snow was 'extreme'. Trouble broke out when the boys began throwing snowballs at each other during the mid-morning break, which Mr Gribble called 'rank disobedience'. He said: 'A letter had been given to the children at the start of the term warning them that throwing snowballs at school was banned. We are responsible for the children's health and safety. They could have been injured if ice was in the snowballs, for example.' But Sharon Dellar, whose 15-year-old son, Ayden Binns, was sent home said: 'I just laughed when Ayden told me what happened, because I couldn't believe it. It's not often we get snow, and I guess they just wanted to have some fun.'

Evening Standard 9/2/07

Heel rage

YEOVIL Town Council has changed its bye-laws on public safety and nuisance grounds to outlaw anything that has wheels and can be attached to the feet. The ban captures the new craze for Heelys as well as skateboards, roller skates and roller blades. Youngsters caught using Heelys in the town centre face being arrested by the police and prosecuted, with a maximum potential fine of £500. In theory, the law means a girl of 12 using her Heelys while out shopping with her parents could be arrested, fined, and left with a criminal record. Yeovil has a particular problem with youths skateboarding and roller-blading because it is built on a hill and provides ideal conditions. Councillor Tony Fife said: 'I think it is also necessary to keep Heelys out of the town. If you get someone aged 14 or 15, who is six feet tall, going 20 miles an hour through the streets in their Heelys, that could cause an awful lot of damage.'

Yeovil Town News 7/2/07

Fizzle fighters

A traditional bonfire built by fire fighters and situated next to a fire station has been scrapped because it could breach Health and Safety regulations. The Guy Fawkes night celebration in Coleshill, Warwickshire, fell foul of new legislation that requires public bonfires to be cordoned off and monitored 24 hours a day. The axe has fallen on the event because Coleshill fire station, on Park Road, is only open during the day and could not provide the security needed to ensure the bonfire was not tampered with. Local fire fighter and town mayor Norman Henderson described the decision as 'legislation gone mad'.

Tamworth Herald 25/10/04

Off the skids

KIDS have been banned from making ice slides in the playground over fears that parents might sue schools. Janitors have been told to pour salt or sawdust on slippery patches in case anyone gets hurt. But education authorities have been accused of 'wrapping children in cotton wool'. Council bosses in Aberdeen, Edinburgh, East Lothian, Angus and North Ayrshire have imposed an outright ban on what they call 'slip hazards' in schools. A spokesman for Edinburgh City Council said: 'Teachers will undertake a risk assessment of the playground to ensure children can play safely, which would mean gritting areas susceptible to icing over.'

The Daily Record 23/1/07

Hair flare

FOR the first time in more than 250 years, children will not be allowed to carry candles at a cathedral service in case their hair catches fire. There is no record of a child going up in flames since 1747 when the Christingle service began at Chelmsford Cathedral. However, children this year will carry fluorescent glowsticks rather than the traditional candles set in oranges. Eric Pickles, the MP for nearby Brentwood and Ongar, criticised the move, saying: 'Health and safety will ban everything. I would be interested to hear when the last time a candle set fire to a child's hair. Eventually, they will work out a way to take all the fun out of Christmas.' But Richard Spilsbury, one of the organisers, said some parents had raised concerns about their children's hair catching fire. 'We thought we would give it a try. They glow quite brightly,' he said.

Daily Telegraph 13/12/06

DO-gooders are out to turn Santa into Satan. Killjoy bosses at the St Elli shopping centre in Llanelli, South Wales, have installed a webcam to spy on their Santa in case he is accused of being a paedophile. Manager Gilmour Jones said: 'It protects both Santa and the children from allegations of abuse. It was either this or not having a Santa's grotto at all. It's a sad sign of the times.' The child protection charity Kidscape added that youngsters should be banned from sitting on Santa's knee. Director Michelle Elliot said: 'Children should not sit on Santa's knee. It's a shame but you can't vet all the people dressed as Santa. There's no need to take the risk.'

The Sun 10/12/04

Ball breaker

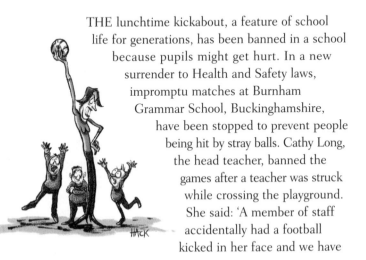

THE lunchtime kickabout, a feature of school life for generations, has been banned in a school because pupils might get hurt. In a new surrender to Health and Safety laws, impromptu matches at Burnham Grammar School, Buckinghamshire, have been stopped to prevent people being hit by stray balls. Cathy Long, the head teacher, banned the games after a teacher was struck while crossing the playground. She said: 'A member of staff accidentally had a football kicked in her face and we have had a few kids having to see matron because they have been whacked with a football.' But Tam Fry from the National Obesity Forum said: 'This is absolutely bananas. In a day and age when children are not getting enough exercise as it is, it seems absolutely ludicrous to effectively tell children they cannot run about during lunch breaks. What are they supposed to do? Sit around and get fat?'

Daily Telegraph 27/1/07

Naughty Bob

KIDDIES' favourite Bob the Builder has come under fire from safety campaigners for flouting safety rules. Bob has been accused of setting a bad example to his young fans – and even endangering the lives of his fellow characters. In one episode, the TV construction worker was condemned for violating seven workplace safety laws, from swinging from the side of his bulldozer, Muck, to walking under heavy equipment dangling from a crane. He doesn't wear a seatbelt when he's driving and allows his pal Wendy to visit his building site without a hard hat on. A spokesman for the Royal Society for the Prevention of Accidents warned: 'Although it's entertainment, it's good if they show good safety practice. A lot of people watch the show so it should be used to prevent accidents.'

The Sun 10/1/02

Cross passengers

BRITISH Airways defended its position in banning check-in worker Nadia Eweida from wearing a crucifix at work, not because it was a religious icon but 'purely on grounds of health and safety', according to the airline's chief executive, Willie Walsh. 'Just to take one simple example,' he told reporters, 'What if an irate passenger in a check-in queue lost his temper and grabbed hold of a cross worn by a member of staff? And then – admittedly in a worst-case scenario – what if the passenger then suffered a severe allergic reaction to the type of metal it was made from? We could be sued for millions!' However, in a separate statement, archbishop Dr Rowan Williams reacted by saying: 'I would question if that is a sensible kind of response.'

Braindead.co.uk 26/11/0

Fire watchers

HUNDREDS of volunteer firefighters are to be banned from putting out fires because of Safety at Work rules. Thirty-two Highland auxiliary 'stations' will be closed as firefighting units following a stormy meeting of the Fire Board. Volunteer crews will be given a fire prevention role, offering advice to householders and schools. But if a house catches fire they will have to stand by and wait for a fully trained, paid crew to arrive from the nearest station, possibly 30 or 45 minutes away. In some cases, as on Evie in the Orkney Isles, the paid firefighters will be travelling from a different island. Eddie Jackson, 48, one of nine volunteers who operate the unit at Glendale, serving a community of about 300 people, said: 'Forcing us to do nothing when a neighbour's chimney is on fire is crazy. We can fight it with water from outside without breathing apparatus and have done for years.' The changes were prompted by criticism from the Health and Safety Executive over working practices and an inspection report which said the 32 units were not needed.

The Times 15/4/05

Poppy cock-up

COUNCILLORS have vowed to fight a Health and Safety ban on a poppy shower at a Remembrance Day service that has been taking place for decades. Fire inspectors told Sandwell Council they could not include the shower in the November 14 service at West Bromwich Town Hall because it could constitute a hazard. The paper poppy shower, part of an annual service attended by war veterans, has been part of West Bromwich Town Hall's Remembrance celebrations since before the Second World War. But Keith Davies of the council said: 'Even if it means I've got to do it myself and take a fire extinguisher, I'm determined it's going to go ahead. Poppies will be falling on November 14. It seems very strange that we have been doing this for the past 60-odd years and all of a sudden, it's a Health and Safety issue.'

The Sun 26/10/04

Fire in the cold

LEWES Bonfire Council has appealed to non-residents to stay away from the Sussex town's bonfire night on the grounds that standing around outdoors in November can be 'an unpleasant experience', and the event will be 'confusing and frightening' for children.

The Times 5/11/04

Stop children crossing

SCHOOLCHILDREN were left to cross a busy road on their own when their lollipop man went off sick – because teachers were banned from helping by Health and Safety zealots. The pupils from Royal High Junior School in Bath – some as young as seven – had to dodge rush-hour traffic after council officials ruled that teachers were not sufficiently trained to take over. But parents accused the pedantic officials of putting their children's lives at risk. One mother, who refused to be named, said: 'I called the council and they told me that for health and safety reasons they couldn't put someone there who hadn't had the proper training. But there were seven-year-olds having to cross the road themselves – it's health and safety gone mad.'

Daily Mail 20/10/06

Xmas tinsel choker

A Bristol secondary school has banned pupils from wearing tinsel to an end-of-term Christmas celebration. Chipping Sodbury School imposed the ban on a non-uniform day because teachers believe tinsel causes litter and could pose a danger if pupils try to strangle each other. Parents and pupils were told of the decision in a newsletter from head teacher Philip Lidstone and deputy head Mel Jeffries, who said that 'health and safety reasons' were behind the ban. Mr Jeffries said: 'We want all of our children to enjoy Christmas and have a good time, but at the same time making sure there are no accidents to spoil it. If tinsel is worn loosely around the neck it can be pulled tight and we want to avoid anything like that.'

Bristol Evening Post 16/12/06

Mind your step

BRISTOL City Council bureaucrats have launched a crackdown
on what they say is the latest dangerous item of homeware: the
doormat. More commonly associated with the humble role of
being somewhere for visitors to wipe their feet, council chiefs
have raised the mat's status to that of 'tripping hazard'. Now they
have banned the floor furnishing and ordered tenants to remove
the offending items or risk having them taken away. But residents
who have received the ultimatum dismissed the idea as 'ludicrous'. The council sent a letter entitled Health and Safety Issues
– Hazardous Mats to thousands of tenants living in flats and
high-rise blocks. It reads: 'During a routine Health and Safety
inspection of the block, it was noted that loose mats were present
in hallways/corridors outside people's flats. These represent a
"tripping hazard" and should be removed immediately. By all
means have your own mats inside your front door, but please do
not leave them outside, creating a risk to others.'

Daily Mail 13/10/06

Conker goggles

A headmaster has introduced safety goggles for his pupils in a bid
to stop the local council banning games of conkers in the playground. Shaun Halfpenny, the head of Cummersdale Primary
School in Cumbria, feared the game would be banned after he
read a council memo warning schools about dangerous breaktime
activities, fearing youngsters could suffer eye injuries if struck by
flying pieces of conker. Pupils are now queueing up try out the
two sets of safety glasses, more commonly used in science lessons.

The Guardian 4/10/04

Pole danger

FIRE chiefs in the Plymouth area are under a blaze of criticism after banning the traditional fireman's pole – because it posed a 'Health and Safety hazard'. Firefighters risk their lives every day, but bosses overseeing the construction of a new £2.4 million station ruled that the poles are too dangerous. It is feared someone might slip off and hurt themselves, get repetitive back strain, turn an ankle or – heaven forbid – suffer severe chafing to the hands and/or thighs. Staff will now have to run down the stairs of the new Greenbank Fire Station in Plymouth, Devon, raising concerns that vital seconds will be lost on their way to a 999 call. Greenbank Station Officer Ken Mulville said: 'It is ludicrous – we were all flabbergasted to find we will have to run down the stairs now.'

Daily Mail 4/8/06

Hard rocks

BRITAIN'S traditional rocking horses, which have their roots in knights practising their jousts, could be crippled by new

European safety regulations (CENLEC). According to the new standards, 'activity toys' cannot have a height from saddle to floor of more than 60 cm (less than two feet). That effectively rules out all but the smallest rocking horses, say craftsmen in the cottage industry's 60 or so firms who comprise the £35m per annum industry.

EU Weekly News 30/11/03

Cakewalk closed

HEALTH and Safety officers have closed Britain's last 'moving staircase' fairground attraction, even though the ride has operated in complete safety for the past 72 years. The owner of the former Butlin's camp at Felixstowe says he believes the cakewalk, which has been running since 1933, is the last one left in Britain. Inspectors from the Health and Safety Executive have ruled that it must be closed because it no longer meets modern safety standards.

Suffolk Evening Star 25/3/05

Kick off

SCHOOLS across Renfrewshire, Scotland, have banned pupils from taking part in after-school football over fears they could be sued for injuries. The games have been banned because volunteer coaches are not covered by the schools' insurance schemes for after-class games.

BBC News 12/3/05

Xmas choker

SAINSBURY'S, the British grocery chain, has cancelled a plan to sell Christmas puddings containing 'lucky sixpences' because Health and Safety Executive regulations say they are a choking hazard. Instead, it will attach the coins to 'collectors' cards' and suggest customers place them under the plate or placemat of a lucky family member.

Daily Telegraph 18/10/05

Bright sparks

EMPLOYERS could be forced to carry out 'risk assessments' on the strength of the sun under proposals from Brussels to protect outdoor workers. Workers would receive training in how to limit their exposure to sunlight, while managers would have to record preventative steps taken by employees – such as wearing shirts and hats. Britain's one million outdoor workers would receive 20 minutes' training a year in how to reduce the risks from sun exposure. Employers would be required to pay for the training, as well as assessing and controlling workers' exposure. The cost to industry would be £8 million over the next ten years, according to the government assessment.

Evening Standard 21/6/05

Give a dog...

NEW European Union rules on food storage could ban butchers giving a dog a bone. City officials in Bradford, West

Yorkshire, have banned butchers from selling dog bones. New Brussels rules class bones as a waste by-product, and butchers must pay for them to be incinerated. Council bureaucrats warned butcher John Smith that he faced losing his licence if he carried on selling them.

The Sun 2/8/05

Steam pressure

VINTAGE steam railways and traction engines are under threat from the EU Hot Surfaces Directive on the protection from steam, hot surfaces and valves. All hot surfaces will have to be insulated, and obtruding objects such as shovels and pipes have to be painted fluorescent yellow. Steam engines will be made impossible to drive.

The Times 3/7/94

Putting the boot in

WELLINGTON boots now come with a 24-page user's manual in accordance with the EU Directive for Personal Protective Equipment 89/696. The booklet is printed in ten languages and gives advice on risk assessment, storage conditions, life expectancy, washing in a mild detergent, and resistance to electricity, cold weather and oil – but not water. Users are advised to try each boot for fitting before use. Even the amount of energy absorbed by the heels is recorded. The manufacturers are required to test their boots twice a month at EU-approved laboratories to ensure that they comply with the standards.

Daily Telegraph 26/5/97

Make and mend

FIREFIGHTERS in the Bristol area are set to be banned
from washing and repairing their own kit by Britain's Health
and Safety Executive following a ruling by European officials.
Traditionally, many firefighters have taken home their tunics,
trousers, gloves and boots and spruced them up ready for the
next day's duties. They have also carried out running repairs
for free. Now the Authority is being recommended to contract
out the repair and maintenance of kit at a cost of nearly
£280 000 a year. EC rules will outlaw repairs and washing by
'untrained people', and will force the Authority to put a quality
control system in place. The rules will also order the Authority
to replace tunics after five years – some are eight years old.

Bristol Evening Post 15/12/99

Shake-up for farmers

THOUSANDS of farmers and other workers are to be banned
from driving tractors, lorries and dumper trucks for much of
the working day under an EU directive on vibrating machinery.
The restrictive limits of the EU Physical Agents (Vibration)
Directive were agreed in Brussels and have been backed by
Britain's Health and Safety Executive. The directive was
immediately condemned by the National Farmers' Union as a
'masterpiece in madness'. The NFU led opposition to the
directive because it meant farmers would have been forbidden
from driving a tractor for more than three to four hours a day.
However, the impact of the law will be even heavier on other
industries. The HSE said it would cost £3 billion to £4.8 billion
to implement. Ben Gill, the NFU president, said: 'This directive

has been driven through without any scientific justification. This is the European nanny state gone mad.' Using an arcane formula to measure the 'whole body vibration', the time limit for using a chainsaw would be one and a half hours. Lorry drivers would be restricted to working for only six hours, and dumper truck drivers to two hours. The time limits for using a road drill would be 47 minutes.

Daily Telegraph 14/3/02

Breaks on trailers

DEFENCE chiefs have been landed with a £21 million bill to fit army trailers with brakes – because they breach EC rules. Brussels bureaucrats are insisting on the change even though thousands of the trailers have been in use without problems. A senior army source said: 'It's true the trailers don't have brakes, but it doesn't matter. They are towed by other vehicles such as Land Rovers, and as long as they are attached properly the risks are tiny.' Another source said: 'This beggars belief. It is complete madness and a disgrace.'

Sunday Mirror 26/6/05

Topple test turnaround

A cash-strapped council has agreed to stump up the money to fix headstones flattened during 'topple tests' after furious protests from campaigners. Gosport councillors have confirmed they will find up to £100 000 to repair the graves after carrying out the controversial safety tests on memorials at the town's Ann's Hill Cemetery. It is welcome news for angry relatives, who objected after seeing cherished gravestones toppled and were then told they had to pay for repairs. The bills sparked a political row. Council bosses had hoped the Health and Safety Executive (HSE) would foot the bill, claiming the tests – designed to prevent anyone being injured from collapsing gravestones – were carried out on HSE advice.

The News, Portsmouth, 14/2/07

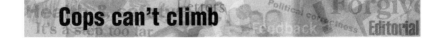

Cops can't climb

A HIGH Court judge criticised the Health and Safety Executive for wasting public time and money on prosecuting the Metropolitan Police Commissioner and his predecessor for failing to warn officers about the danger of climbing on roofs. Following separate incidents in which one police officer died and another was injured after falling through roofs while on duty, top police brass faced criminal charges of failure to warn, which ended most recently in acquittal on some charges and a hung jury on others after £1 million in lawyers' fees and a further £2 million in investigations. Had the HSE succeeded, the Met had planned to instruct its officers not to climb above head height. 'It would have been a veritable burglars' charter, a victory for criminals, and would have encouraged suspects to use roofs to escape,' said one senior officer.

Daily Telegraph 30/6/03

Cake ban overturned

ELDERLY patients can continue to enjoy their afternoon treat of home-baked goods from the Women's Institute after a hospital ban on the cakes was lifted. The WI said they were 'delighted' to learn the ban on their cakes – on the grounds they could pose a health risk – had been overturned. There was uproar when health bosses decided cakes made by the Radwinter WI in Essex could prove potentially dangerous to elderly patients. The group baked 12 cakes a month for patients at Saffron Walden Community Hospital as a treat for afternoon tea. But then Uttlesford Primary Care Trust decided to stop the supply of cakes because they it could not guarantee the patients' safety without inspecting the kitchens where they were baked.

Daily Mail 30/7/04

Killjoy Christmas

A council has ordered staff not to put up Christmas decorations in the office in case they get hurt. Killjoy bosses have also banned festive lights because they are too costly to run. Staff at Tower Hamlets Council in East London were stunned when safety busybodies issued the order. One worker said: 'We only wanted to get into the spirit and brighten the place up. It feels more like the Eastern bloc than the East End round here now – except slightly less cheery.' A council spokeswoman said: 'There's a concern people might hurt themselves trying to attach hanging decorations from the ceiling.'

Staff were also told drawing pins would ruin newly decorated ceilings. Unlit trees on desks and cabinets are allowed.

The Sun 24/11/06

Mind your step

FIREFIGHTERS on Humberside have been told by their employers that it is dangerous for them to go up ladders. Given that going up ladders to rescue people from blazing buildings is what firefighters do for a living, the news has been greeted with more than a spark of incredulity by the individuals who man the fire service for Hull and its surrounding area. But it is not sending up extending ladders on the back of fire engines to deal with towering infernos that is causing concern. It is climbing mere stepladders to install smoke alarms in people's homes, a popular prevention measure offered free by the Humberside Fire and Rescue Service. The brigade is reviewing its stepladder policy after local officials of the Fire Brigades Union pointed out that a firefighter on a stepladder not much more than 6 ft from the floor may be contravening the Health and Safety Executive Work at Height Regulations 2005.

The Times 18/1/07

Author pulls book in paper cut fear

THE author of a book honouring First World War soldiers has been told he needs £5m worth of insurance to sell them on council premises. The cover Mark Sutton needs is to protect against people dropping books on their feet or getting a paper cut and then suing the council. He says the council's demand goes against everything the men in the book, Tell Them of Us, stood for. But Swindon Council spokeswoman Victoria Tagg said the insurance was necessary to protect against potential claims. 'All suppliers of services and products to Swindon Council must have public liability insurance,' she said. 'The cover we require is normally for £5m, but we are prepared to reduce this to £2m for some smaller suppliers.' The book has now been taken off the shelves. Mark, 44, said: 'It's crazy. I refuse to get the insurance. I'm not going to bow down to it. It's against the principles of what I wrote the book for. It's just another one of these silly Health and Safety measures and it has gone potty.'

Swindon Advertiser 22/2/07

About the author

Alan Pearce was born in London and has worked as a journalist, broadcaster and author for the past 30 years. A former managing editor at both the *International Press Institute* and *The Phnom Penh Post*, and foreign correspondent, he has first-hand experience of Health and Safety issues, covering conflicts around the world for a variety of news organisations, including the BBC, *Time* magazine, *The Times*, *Sunday Times*, *Sunday Telegraph*, *Paris Match*, and *Sygma Photo News* agency. He is married with one daughter and divides his time between London and southwest France.